Power in the Senate

RANDALL B. RIPLEY

Power
in the Senate

ST. MARTIN'S PRESS   New York

28611

PREFACE

In the recent surge of congressional research, the House of Representatives has received considerably more attention than the Senate. This book is an attempt to correct the imbalance. The central purpose of this volume is to analyze the internal distribution of power in the Senate and the consequences of that distribution.

The Senate is viewed here as an institution. Some of its relations with other institutions and systems are explored. But, principally, its internal processes are analyzed, and some of the consequences of different patterns of internal processes for policy examined.

In Part I three general models of power distribution are presented, the development of the principal institutional competitors for power since 1869 is sketched, and the transition from one pattern of power distribution to another in the years between 1945 and the present (1968) is treated in some detail. In Part II the distribution of power in the contemporary Senate (defined as the middle and late 1960's) is described and analyzed in considerable detail. In Part III the principal consequences of the distribution of power in the contemporary Senate are analyzed.

Although not all the relationships are discussed systematically in this book, it is important to remember that what the Senate does is intimately related to election results, public opinion, national and international events, interest groups, the House of Representatives, the President, his political appointees, and the permanent bureaucracy.

It is hoped that the present study will eventually provide part of the foundation for a more general assessment of Congress's impact on policy and its responsiveness to the public interest. The present aim is more limited: to understand the major alternative patterns of internal power distribution in the Senate. Questions are raised about the values inherent in the alternatives, but there is no attempt to prescribe how the Senate *should* distribute power internally.

A number of my former colleagues at the Brookings Institution read all or most of several early drafts of this volume and aided me with their comments. I am particularly indebted to James L. Sundquist, Gilbert Y. Steiner, Stephen Horn, and George A. Graham. My wife, Vivian Usher Ripley, also read and commented insightfully on the manuscript. My colleagues in the Department of Political Science at The Ohio State University reacted helpfully to a paper drawn from Chapters 1 and 3 that I presented at a departmental colloquium.

I wish to thank the Brookings Institution for sponsoring the round table meetings described in Appendix A and for giving me access to the transcripts of those meetings. Brookings is, of course, not responsible for my use or interpretation of the material in those transcripts. Professor Frederic N. Cleaveland of the University of North Carolina and I jointly planned the meetings and prepared the discussion outlines. I am grateful to the senators and Senate staff members who attended these meetings and spoke so candidly and lucidly. I am also grateful to the additional senators and staff members who granted me personal interviews. Without these men and women willing to interrupt very busy schedules, this book obviously could never have been written.

Finally, and most important, I wish to dedicate this book to my wife and son, who make life enjoyable.

CONTENTS

PART

The Distribution of Power in the Senate

Chapter 1: **Introduction** [1]

In order to achieve and maintain great impact on public policy, the United States Congress needs to distribute internal power in such a way as to promote efficient activity, ready access to the most influential points in the legislative process, a relatively steady stream of output, and a relatively high degree of institutional stability. In order to maximize its responsiveness to the public interest at the same time, Congress needs to promote thoroughness, rationality, representativeness, and responsibility in considering legislative proposals.[2]

3

THE NATURE OF SENATORIAL POWER

There is no agreement in the literature on how to measure power in the Senate, or even how to conceive of it. Some, for example, have inferred power relationships from roll-call votes; others are skeptical of the possibility of doing so.[3] This volume does not propose an exact measure of power. What it does offer is a two-sided perspective on power in the Senate.

Power involves a relationship between at least two individuals. Senator A is powerful (or influential) to the extent that he can induce Senator B to behave in some way in which Senator B would not behave of his own volition.[4] Occasionally, a senator can appear to wield power unopposed: that is, he defines the desired impact and no one opposes his wishes. But, in reality, he is probably unopposed either because he is stating an uncontroversial position, in which case power is not involved, or because silence or lack of opposition is at least an implicit recognition of his power. A senator's power over other senators comes from two principal sources: his personal skills and expertise and his institutional position or positions.[5]

Personal power may develop because a senator is charming or skillful at personal relations. It may develop because he possesses real expertise on specific subject matters. Senators can and do develop power of this sort regardless of their position or lack of position in the various institutional hierarchies of the Senate.

Institutional power comes from holding institutional positions that are presumed to have some power attached to them and/or place the holder in a strategic position in relation to substantive matters. Party leaders and committee chairmen, for example, almost surely possess some institutional power.[6]

The two types of power complement each other. If a senator possesses personal skills that he can use to achieve the desired impact on legislative results, his power is still greatly enhanced when he achieves an important institutional position. And he is likely to use his personal skills to make the most out of his institutional position. On the other hand, if a person comes to a powerful institutional position before he acquires much personal power, he can still develop such power and enhance his total impact on legislative results.[7]

The use of legislative power can be either direct or indirect. A senator can take a position on a specific legislative issue and can work to implement his position. In this case, he acts directly on the issue at hand. Many senators have considerable power on a few specific issue areas but are relatively powerless on other matters. Thus, in many situations, it is meaningless to say that Senator X is powerful legislatively unless the area in which he exercises power is specified. A few senators, such as active and aggressive party leaders, however, may develop general legislative power.

Powerful senators may also have an impact on internal organizational questions that face the Senate. By having the greatest influence on these decisions, a senator is often indirectly affecting future legislative outcomes. For example, southern senators who used their power to maintain the filibuster with minimal limits were, at the same time, having an impact on the possibility of civil rights legislation. A senator who uses his power to support a given candidate for a party leadership position is doing so, in part, because he expects that leader to work for desirable substantive measures. If a senator urges changes in the seniority practices of the Senate, he does so because he expects that the changes will lead to desirable legislative results.

How can changing patterns of institutional power and personal power distribution be ascertained? Institutional positions that are thought to carry power with them can easily be identified, and the distribution of these positions can then be analyzed. Personal power presents a more difficult problem. There are two major possible ways of finding out about personal power. One is to rely on the reputations for personal power that knowledgeable first-hand observers, often journalists, attribute to various individual senators and groups of senators. A second is to probe the perceptions that senators (and staff members) themselves have both of the power of others and of their own efficacy in achieving the legislative goals they favor. Evidence of all three varieties—on institutional positions, on reputations for power, and on senators' perceptions of their own legislative power and that of others—is useful.

THREE MODELS OF POWER DISTRIBUTION

Although the power of individual senators is a meaningful subject of inquiry, it is also important to ascertain the power of different groups or coalitions of senators. These groups or coalitions may be of several types: ideological, partisan, regional, or institutional.

There has been a wide variety of different coalitions based on ideology, party, and region since the Civil War, but the three major institutional competitors for power have remained the same. These are the party leaders, senior members of the standing committees (particularly the chairmen), and all senators (especially in their roles as subcommittee chairmen). To understand the nature and impact of the relations between these competitors, three models of power distribution in the Senate will be employed.

Models of political behavior are useful because they suggest inter-relationships, not because they portray pure types that occur precisely as described. Over the last hundred years in the Senate three basic patterns of power distribution have emerged. These are designated as *centralization, decentralization,* and *individualism.* Each label suggests where the principal legislative power is located: with the central party leader or leaders in the first case, with the standing committee chairmen in the second case, or, in the third case, with the individual senators (often as subcommittee chairmen).

These categories do not represent a simple distinction between rule by the one, the few, and the many. Rather they represent degrees of rule by the few. If the party leaders hold the most power, there are likely to be several of them; and they do not, of course, hold *all* power. If the standing committee chairmen hold more power than the other competitors, the number of the few who make the most important substantive and institutional decisions is increased. Power is shared unevenly by these few, and they do not monopolize all power in the Senate. If all or almost all senators as individuals share in important ways in the principal decisions that the Senate makes, they do not share power democratically; on any specific decision some of the senators are going to be more powerful than others.[8]

Widespread support for change or reform of institutional arrangements in the Senate is not highly likely in any of the three models. An unusual combination of circumstances is necessary to motivate members to institute and direct change. Incremental change, however, is inevitable because of personnel changes and a fluctuating environment. Every senator's instinct is to seek power, and the way to power lies in maximizing individualistic tendencies in the Senate. The greater the degree of centralization present, therefore, the greater the chance that organized change or reform (in the direction of less centralization) will succeed.

Senators already in an individualistic situation are unlikely to support changes except those that will even further proliferate power to the individual. Thus, for example, support for more staff members responsible to individual senators can be expected. Proposals designed to bring more advance notice and orderliness to floor proceedings might also be attractive because such measures would provide an individual senator with a clearer indication of when he should be present on the floor to protect his interests.

Centralization

THE DISTRIBUTION OF POWER TO PARTY LEADERS AND STANDING COMMITTEES. When centralization is present, the power holders in both parties are clearly identifiable. Usually they hold the principal formal titles: Majority Leader and Minority Leader, Majority Whip and Minority Whip, chairman of the Policy or Steering Committee, and chairman of the conference. Once the leaders are elected or appointed to their positions, they consult with some other members of their party, but they are free to adopt legislative positions largely on their own. The leaders assume aggressive roles and work actively for a united party.

Party committees or the party conference (the full membership of the Senate party), if used on legislative matters, are under the firm direction of the leaders. They do not develop independent weight that would enable them to challenge the legislative positions espoused by the leaders.

Since approximately 1913, the leaders of a centralized party have worked closely with a President of their party on all major legislative matters. These leaders think of themselves as his lieutenants, and he becomes a major centralizing force. Party members feel that party is legitimately the highest organ for taking policy positions. These positions are considered to be binding on all members of the party unless highly unusual circumstances intervene.

Assignment of members to the most important standing committees are used to reward the faithful, with the party leader or leaders controlling a centralized assignment process. Seniority may be a criterion for committee assignments, but it is not the only one.

These committee chairmen and ranking minority members act as close and loyal lieutenants of the central party leader or leaders. The chairmen and, to a lesser extent, ranking minority members have great power inside their committees. For example, they can decide whether or not to appoint standing subcommittees. If they choose to appoint subcommittees, they carefully control the individual appointments to them. They supervise the substantive output of the committees and subcommittees in accord with the principles of the party program and the wishes and needs of the party leaders. In addition, they work for party goals in conference committees.

Committees and subcommittees work more closely with the party leaders than with interest groups or bureaus of the executive branch, although the latter two participants in the legislative process can persuade the leaders and thus influence the committees. The standing committee system is highly valued by many members specifically because it is an adjunct of the party.

CONSEQUENCES OF THE DISTRIBUTION OF POWER. In a centralized situation the individual senator is party-oriented. If he wishes to accomplish his legislative aims, he must enlist the support of the central party leaders and their loyal lieutenants, the committee chairmen or ranking minority members.

Staff members attached to the central leaders and possibly to some of the key committee chairmen may be important in the legislative operations of a centralized Senate, but they are not likely to develop independent power. Most staff members perform routine tasks.

The party leaders are familiar with the substance and status of the major bills in the Senate at any given time. They have a sense of priorities and a reasonably orderly plan for bringing matters to the floor. They consult closely and constantly with committee leaders in planning a steady flow of work to the Senate floor. The Senate's legislative process is unified: both the informational and command functions are clearly in the hands of the central party leaders.

Decentralization

THE DISTRIBUTION OF POWER TO PARTY LEADERS AND STANDING COMMITTEES. When decentralization is the dominant pattern, the titular party leaders are not necessarily the real leaders. The members usually look to committee, regional, or ideological bloc leaders in addition to the central party leaders for their cues on legislative positions. The formal leaders, once elected, consult a number of members of their party and are heavily influenced by key members. In a decentralized situation the formal leaders play a large, but not commanding, role in determining party positions on legislation. They are aggressive only occasionally in seeking to influence important legislative matters. Party committees or conferences, if used for legislative purposes, however, may have independently powerful leaders chairing or sitting on them. This situation leads to occasional policy clashes with the formal party leaders.

The leaders of the President's party work with the President on some major legislative matters, usually acting as his lieutenants, but their adherence is often conditional. They are also willing to express their own dissent from his position or to transmit the dissenting views of other senators to him.

The individual senators view party as an important organ for taking legislative positions that should frequently be supported by most members. But there is no widespread assumption that party positions are binding on the members or that party positions should be taken on all major items on the legislative agenda.

Committee assignments are used to reward those senators personally close to the assigning authorities. Seniority is also an important criterion for committee assignment. Committee chairmen and ranking minority members tend to become the most powerful figures in the Senate. Some consider themselves allies of the central leaders; some generally pit themselves against the leaders on most policy questions. Chairmen have great power within their committees. Sometimes they strive to control subcommittee structure and output (as well as full committee output) for the good of the party. But if they are in disagreement with the majority of the party, they may try to control the output of their committees and subcommittees in ways inimical to the party.

In a decentralized Senate, individual committees and subcommittees may work more closely with interest groups and pieces of the executive branch than with party leaders. Senators feel that the committee system is valuable because it allows subject matter expertise to develop unfettered by strict party control.

CONSEQUENCES OF THE DISTRIBUTION OF POWER. In a decentralized situation, the individual senator tends to be committee-oriented. If he wants to have legislative impact, the key supporters he needs are committee chairmen or ranking minority members.

Staff members attached to the most important committees, subcommittees, and individual members (especially chairmen and ranking minority members) may develop independent power in the legislative process. Most personal and committee staff members perform only routine tasks.

The party leader or leaders have a general impression of what bills are at what stage in the legislative process. However, they have no particularly compelling plan for bringing legislation to the floor. Usually the committee chairmen tell the leaders when they would like important business scheduled and the leaders comply, seeking only to maintain an orderly flow of business to the floor. The legislative process is partially unified because the informational function is controlled by the central party leader or leaders. It is also partially segmented because there is no centrally located command function.

Individualism

THE DISTRIBUTION OF POWER TO PARTY LEADERS AND STANDING COMMITTEES. When individualism prevails in the Senate, the titular party leaders are not necessarily the real leaders. A large number of members can be legitimately referred to as "leaders." The formal central party leaders must consult with a large number of members before they feel free to state positions for the party. These leaders are far less aggressive than leaders in centralized or decentralized Senates, and they play only a limited role in trying to promote a united party on important substantive questions.

Party committees and the party conference are likely to develop independent weight, and the chairmen or other members of these committees will be leaders in their own right. The party committees or conferences often clash with the leaders' policy preferences and often prevail over them.

The central leaders of the President's party meet with him and discuss major legislation. These leaders usually support the President's position verbally; but they are also willing to express their own dissent freely or to transmit that of other senators to him.

Members feel that party is an organ which has some importance in taking policy positions which should sometimes be supported by most members. There is no feeling, however, that the party should always take a position when a major bill is before the Senate or that the members are bound to support the party positions when taken.

Assignments to standing committees are used to reward those senators personally close to the assigning authorities, many of whom are not formal party leaders or even loyal party members. Seniority is also an important criterion for making assignments. Committee assignments thus do not reinforce party loyalty.

Committee chairmen and ranking minority members become independent power centers, although not as powerful as in a decentralized Senate. Their power is not based on alliance or nonalliance with the central party leaders. Chairmen have power inside their committees; but committees also have powerful subcommittee chairmen who are not responsible to the full committee chairmen or to the party leaders. There is no presumption that chairmen will work for party-oriented legislative results. Subcommittee chairmen and ranking minority members of subcommittees are the key legislative figures in the Senate, regardless of their ideological stance or degree of loyalty to party.

In an individualistic situation, the committees and subcommittees work closely on substantive matters with interest groups or individual executive branch agencies. The party leaders become involved in the substantive work of only those committees on which they sit.

Members of an individualized Senate hold the committee system in high esteem because it provides every senator a niche in which he can exercise power, unfettered by any controlling agency.

CONSEQUENCES OF THE DISTRIBUTION OF POWER. In an individualistic situation the individual senator is self-oriented or subcommittee-oriented. His positions on substantive matters in his legislative niche are usually accepted by the whole Senate. Thus he can concentrate on seeking the niche he desires and on maximizing the power available to him.

Personal and committee staff members attached to many senators and committees and subcommittees are important and may develop substantial independent power in dealing with specific subjects.

The party leaders have some information on what bills are at what stage in the legislative process. They employ no general plan for bringing bills to the floor in a given order or at a given time. In any case, work on the floor is not likely to be evenly spaced. Usually the leaders simply accept the scheduling and substantive preferences of committee and subcommittee chairmen. The legislative process as a whole in the Senate appears highly segmented because there is no centrally located command function, and even the informational function is dispersed.

The Three Models Compared

Table I summarizes the most important differences between the three models.

THE THREE MODELS IN HISTORY

Change is difficult to measure in any legislative body.[9] The problem for the Senate is complicated by missing or incomplete data for many periods in the past. Both quantitative and qualitative data are scarce, especially if exact comparability is sought for all Senates since 1869.

TABLE I: POWER IN THE SENATE: THREE MODELS

COMPETITORS FOR POWER	PATTERN OF POWER DISTRIBUTION		
	Centralization	Decentralization	Individualism
Central party leadership	Powerful and aggressive	Moderately powerful and aggresssive	Relatively powerless; unaggressive
Standing committee chairmen	Loyal to the party leaders; moderately powerful	Not necessarily allied with party leadership; independently powerful	Often independent of party leaders; moderately powerful
The individual senator	Party-oriented; relatively powerless	Committee-oriented; relatively powerless	Subcommittee- or self-oriented; relatively powerful
CONSEQUENCES			
Nature of the legislative process	Unified	Partially unified; partially segmented	Segmented
Power acquired by staff members	Low, confined to a few	Moderate; relatively confined	High; relatively widespread
The prospects of organized institutional change (reform)	Most likely	Moderately likely	Least likely

This study uses a variety of data from scholarly commentaries, newspapers, biographies, autobiographies and memoirs, documents, interviews with senators and staff members, and the transcripts of fourteen round table discussion meetings held between April and August, 1965.[10] Some of the judgments based on these data are tentative and, as more data are collected by others, may need to be revised; however, the data are sufficient to support two generalizations: since the Civil War the Senate has approximated each of the three models on at least several occasions, and the present Senate approximates the individualistic model quite closely.

Secondary literature supports the following suggestive chronology: [11]

1869-1885   Individualism
1885-1905   Centralization
1905-1911   Decentralization
1911-1917   Centralization
1917-1933   Individualism
1933-1937   Centralization
1937-1955   Decentralization
1955-1961   Decentralization/individualism (period of transition)
1961-   Individualism

Both parties tend to distribute power in the same way at the same time, which suggests that there are institutional factors at work that transcend party. There are, however, short periods during which the parties differ in the way they distribute power. For example, between 1911 and 1913 the Democrats had a centralized pattern and the Republicans had an individualized pattern. But since the legislative momentum in those years was on the side of the Democrats (although they did not formally become a majority until 1913), those years are included in a period of centralization. In general, when the majority and minority follow different patterns, the majority party pattern is used for classifying the years in question, since legislative momentum generally rests with that party.

The Senate naturally gravitates toward individualism. Changes generated by large numbers of senators are almost always aimed at spreading power. However, changes in the Senate are also generated by its environment. The three times that the Senate has abandoned a pattern of individualism or a pattern of decentralization for a pattern of centralization—in 1885, 1911-1913, and 1933—outside events help explain the reversal of the normal drive for spreading power. In 1885 a combination of events and personalities both inside and outside produced a centralized Senate. In 1911-1913 there was widespread popular agitation for action that seemed to require a centralized Senate. Woodrow Wilson as President aided the movement to centralization. In addition, there was considerable interest in reform and reorganization in the Senate, especially among younger Democrats. In 1933 the impact of the depression and of the new President, Franklin Roosevelt, both contributed to the centralization of power in the Senate. Historical experience suggests that the present pattern of individualism is not likely to be changed wholly by considerations and forces internal to the Senate.

THE SENATE AND ITS ENVIRONMENT

The Senate is important ultimately because it helps make public policy. It does not make policy by itself but, given both its formal constitutional powers and other powers it has developed, it often has an important policy impact. One goal of this study is to provide an analysis of the Senate that can contribute to a broad explanation of where the Senate fits in the larger policy process. The hope is to provide part of the empirical grounding upon which a larger study would have to be based.

The place of the Senate in relation to public policy can be seen more clearly if three different kinds of variables that help explain public policy outcomes are distinguished. The outcomes in turn influence the nature of the variables, as illustrated in the following diagram.[12]

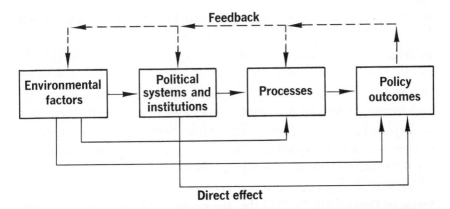

Environmental factors include the basic social and economic structure of the nation, as well as specific events both international and national. Political systems and institutions include the electoral system, the party system, the pressure group system, and the basic institutions of the national government. Processes are essentially the complex set of relations within and between systems and institutions. Policy outcomes are both statutes and administrative decisions. Eventually, the impact of the Senate on public policy will have to be seen in the light of all factors.

The argument in this volume is that what the Senate does internally has external consequences and repercussions for policy. A number of these consequences will be discussed; others will be only alluded to. No one of the three models of power distribution is portrayed as "best." Each has some benefits for some of the numerous participants in the policy process, including both the senators themselves and the public at large, and each has some costs for some of the participants.

Notes

[1] Parts of Chapter 1 and Chapter 3 originally appeared in an article in the May, 1969 *Journal of Politics.* I wish to thank the *Journal of Politics* for permission to use that material here.

[2] The term "public interest" is not used here to denote an absolute concept of what is good for the public apart from what the majority of the public desires. Since much debate over policy is carried on in terms of the "public interest" the notion can perform a consensus-building function. When consensus is achieved on a given goal or goals then the public interest has been identified behaviorally. No precise measurement of consensus is put forth here, although it is certainly plausible to argue that such a measurement could be made by sophisticated use of poll and election data. For one such attempt at measurement see James L. Sundquist, *Politics and Policy* (Brookings, 1968). For a philosophical defense of this limited notion of the public interest see Douglas Price, "Theories of the Public Interest," in Lynton K. Caldwell (ed.), *Politics and Public Affairs* (Institute of Training for Public Service, Indiana University, 1962), pp. 141-159.

[3] For differing positions on this question see David B. Truman, *The Congressional Party* (Wiley, 1959); Robert A. Dahl, "The Concept of Power," *Behavioral Science,* Vol. 2 (July 1957), pp. 201-215; and Duncan MacRae, Jr. and Hugh D. Price, "Scale Positions and 'Power' in the Senate," *Behavioral Science,* Vol. 4 (July 1959), pp. 212-218.

[4] There is, of course, an extensive literature that discusses power and influence and, in many cases, distinguishes between them. For present purposes there seemed to be no reason to distinguish between power and influence. The relatively simple conception of power used here resembles the conception of influence in Robert A. Dahl, *Modern Political Analysis* (Prentice-Hall, 1963), pp. 40-41. A similar conception is presented in Barry E. Collins and Harold Guetzkow, *A Social Psychology of Group Processes for Decision-Making* (Wiley, 1964), p. 121: "When the acts of an agent can (actually or potentially) modify the behavior of a person, or group of persons, the agent has power over that person or group of persons." See chapters 6-8 of Collins and Guetzkow for a number of propositions that might prove fruitful in a more formal analysis of power in the Senate.

[5] Senators may also wield power outside of the Senate. They may be in a position to influence the public or a segment of it, bureaucrats, interest groups, members of the House, or the President. This power may come from a variety of sources.

[6] Truman, in *The Congressional Party,* argues persuasively that this is the case for both the formal party leaders and the committee leaders ("seniority leaders" is his phrase). For data on the formal party leaders in ten Congresses in this century see Randall B. Ripley, *Majority Party Leadership in Congress* (Little, Brown, 1969).

[7] Despite the links between the two types of power (power based on differ-

ent sources, to be more precise) it is worthwhile to keep them separate for analytical purposes. Otherwise, problems of evidence are unnecessarily complicated.

³ In some ways the three models proposed here are analogous to the three general types of coordination process described in Charles E. Lindblom, *The Intelligence of Democracy* (Free Press, 1965), pp. 25-28. He calls these centrally regulated complex decision-making (a hierarchical system analogous to the centralized distribution of power described here); complex decision-making through mutual adjustment (analogous to individualistic distribution of power); and mixed central and noncentral coordination (analogous to decentralized distribution of power).

For some interesting theoretical work also related to the central problem of this study and the Lindblom models see Steven J. Brams, "Measuring the Concentration of Power in Political Systems," *American Political Science Review*, Vol. 62 (June 1968), pp. 461-475. If his ideas could be operationalized meaningfully for the Senate they would offer the hope of a measure of concentration or dispersion of power that could be used to test the ideas presented here.

⁹ For a pioneering effort on the House of Representatives, see Nelson W. Polsby, "The Institutionalization of the U.S. House of Representatives," *American Political Science Review*, Vol. 62 (March 1968), pp. 144-168. See also Randall B. Ripley, *Party Leaders in the House of Representatives* (Brookings, 1967), pp. 49-53.

¹⁰ See Appendix A for a discussion of these meetings and the participants in them.

¹¹ See Appendix B for a short discussion of the principal secondary sources on which the judgments represented by this chronology are based.

¹² The following diagram is adapted from James A. Robinson, "The Major Problems of Political Science," *Politics and Public Affairs*, p. 173. Obviously this diagram and very brief discussion of a policy system are meant only to be illustrative. There is a rapidly developing literature on both policy and systems theory that should be consulted by those interested. See, for example, Austin Ranney, ed., *Political Science and Public Policy* (Markham, 1968) and David Easton, *A Systems Analysis of Political Life* (Wiley, 1965).

Chapter 2: Competitors for Power: The Development of Party Leadership and Standing Committees

A major motive force for changes in the distribution of power in the Senate has been the competition between the party leaders on the one hand and the standing committees and subcommittees on the other. The leaders and the standing committees and subcommittees are also capable of considerable cooperative activity: the committees produce substantive results and the leaders work for their enactment.

But some leaders also seek substantive impact. Even in a highly decentralized Senate, the parties are anxious to keep some form of working control over important standing committees. They have, for example, violated seniority occasionally to maintain such control.[1] Both parties have recently made modifications in the use of the seniority standard for initial assignments to committees.[2]

Some committee and subcommittee members, particularly the senior ones, seek to overrule leaders on scheduling and on matters of party organization. The junior senators avoid these conflicts and instead try to carve out for themselves niches of legislative influence that are protected from the demands and preferences of both the leaders and the senior committee members.

There is always tension between party leaders and individuals in their committee and subcommittee roles. Those individuals who prevail at any given time determine which of the three models of power distribution the Senate most closely approximates. An overview of the development of the institutional positions that have afforded the major competitors part of their power base is important for an understanding of this point.

THE DEVELOPMENT OF THE STANDING COMMITTEE SYSTEM IN THE SENATE

Throughout the history of the Senate, the place of the standing committees has been constantly changing. In general, their impact on substance has grown. The party leaders have generally sought to control the committees; the committees have generally sought autonomy.

Until 1816 the Senate had no standing committees.[3] Instead, special committees were appointed and conducted whatever business the Senate felt it could not handle as a whole. In late 1816 the Senate authorized eleven standing committees. Until 1823 the members of these committees were chosen by ballot by the whole Senate. From 1823 to 1833 the method of choice alternated between ballot, appointment by the President pro tempore of the Senate, and, for one short period, appointment by the Vice-President. During much of the period before 1833 seniority for initial assignments and for rank on committees was so unimportant that chairmenships were rotated.

After 1833 the Senate again resorted to balloting for all members. Chairmenships ceased to rotate, and party control of assignments began to appear. Committees began to divide on predictable ideological lines, and minority reports began to be written. Party control was firm enough by 1846 that, although the formal requirement of balloting remained, the committee assignment lists supplied by the parties were routinely approved.

As the old parties split under the strain of dealing with the slavery question, the Senate found committee assignments more difficult to make. From 1849 to 1857 the President pro tempore again became the appointing agent, although the parties did not relinquish their influence. The southern Democrats dominated the committee chairmanships, and supported the hardening of seniority to protect their position so that they could defend slavery. Democrats defended a version of the principle of seniority (not removing sitting committee members because of their experience) in an 1857 debate over proposed committee assignments. The Republicans had challenged the assignments as unfair; they had not been consulted by the Democrats when the assignments were made.[4] When the Republicans became the majority in the Senate they consulted the Democrats in 1861 but then ceased consulting them, instead filling all committee places themselves. This situation prevailed until the Democrats became numerous enough after the war to force, in effect, the adoption of a seniority criterion.

The number of standing committees grew so large in the late nineteenth and early twentieth centuries that some of the unimportant ones were even chaired by minority party members. Others never met. In 1921 and again in 1946 the Senate pared the number of its committees.

Throughout the post-Civil War period the important committees developed reputations for real expertise and became the primary units of Congress that make a substantive input on legislation. Before roughly 1900-1913, the central leaders could also make an impact on legislation. But since the President has become active in the legislative process and the amount and complexity of business handled by the federal government has grown dramatically, the leaders' substantive role has dwindled.

THE DEVELOPMENT OF SENATE PARTY LEADERSHIP

The Senate party leaders and party committees and machinery largely under their control perform six major functions. First, they help organize the party internally. Second, they schedule the business of the Senate. Third, they seek to have enough senators on the floor when voting occurs to win. Fourth, they collect from and distribute to individual senators a variety of information about substance, scheduling, and the intentions of various participants in the legislative process. Fifth, they attempt to persuade senators to follow their lead. Finally, they maintain liaison with the White House.

Not all party leaders are equally aggressive and consistent in performing these functions. But the more important leaders and party organs perform a number of them in all Congresses. The less important leaders perform only a few of them. The impact of these functions, if performed vigorously, can be to centralize the power of the Senate in the hands of the leaders.

The Floor Leaders

Not until the mid-1880's did the floor leaders of the two parties emerge as active and important officials, although before then there were occasional individual senators who stood out as influential men. Since that time the men holding the principal formal leadership positions have, with only a few exceptions, been active and important. Floor leaders are not, however, automatically invested with a specific quota of power; they must still create much of their own.

Before the Civil War there were no easily identified floor leaders in the Senate and no formally elected party leaders.[5] Individual senators emerged as intellectual leaders or leading debaters only on specific issues. There were no party committees to help schedule the business of the Senate, take party positions, or assign senators to the standing committees. The voting of senators showed no particular party patterns; sectional influences predominated.[6] Before 1828 especially, parties were weak. As the leading commentator on the pre-1828 period put it, in characterizing the state of parties in both houses, "It is the weakness of parties, not their strength, that emerges as the paramount historical fact. Parties on the Hill were largely unorganized groups."[7]

Between 1829 and the beginning of the last pre-Civil War crisis in Congress (about 1849) party leadership became more significant. It was during this period, for example, (in 1846) that party control of committee assignments first appeared. Within a few years, however, the fracturing of the prewar parties made the status of party control dubious.[8]

During the Civil War, the Republican party, controlled by the radicals, emerged as a relatively strong force in the Senate. No single senator stood out as leader, however; in fact, in many ways the dominating figure in both houses was a representative, Thaddeus Stevens of Pennsylvania. During this period, the Republican party not only possessed organizational importance but also began to take positions on substantive questions. Party members were expected to adopt these positions as their own.

But as soon as the urgencies of war and reconstruction had passed, party discipline on questions of policy quickly vanished.[9] Between 1869 and 1885 neither party was governed by consistently active and powerful leaders, and periods of activity alternated with periods of lethargy. The Republicans elected a chairman of their caucus who was assumed to be the party's floor leader. They occasionally used the caucus for legislative purposes, created a Committee on Committees, and developed a Steering Committee to help with scheduling. However, the only Republican leader before 1885 who developed much power was Roscoe Conkling of New York, who did not hold the formal position of chairman of the caucus.

He derived power from personal traits rather than institutional position, and he was not always successful legislatively.[10]

The post-War Democrats, almost always in the minority, also developed formal positions. The chairman of their caucus was their floor leader. They too had a Committee on Committees and developed what amounted to a steering committee when they came into the majority for two years between 1879 and 1881.

It was precisely this Senate that Woodrow Wilson described in *Congressional Government*, published in 1885:

The public now and again picks out here and there a Senator who seems to act and speak with true instinct of statesmanship and who unmistakably merits the confidence of colleagues and of people. But such a man, however eminent, is never more than *a* Senator. No one is *the* Senator. No one may speak for his party as well as for himself; no one exercises the special trust of acknowledged leadership.[11]

After 1885 it still was not clear that the floor leader would develop power. Indeed, it was not always clear which men were floor leaders; some individuals were called floor leaders without formally bearing a title. The practice of electing a single Majority Leader or Minority Leader who would serve during an entire Congress and presumably would be reelected did not become established until the period between 1911 and 1913.

Both parties did elect chairmen of their caucuses before 1911, but these men were not always important leaders. For example, from 1885 to 1897 the Republicans had two different caucus chairmen, George Edmunds of Vermont and John Sherman of Ohio, but neither was a major figure in the party.

Thus until roughly 1911-1913, the real party leaders were not necessarily the formal floor leaders or caucus chairmen. Only since 1911-1913 has it become customary for actual and potential power to reside in the titled Majority Leader or Minority Leader.

The Republican party in the Senate was blessed with its most effective leaders ever from 1885 to 1911. The leadership group shifted from year to year with the changing membership of the

Senate, but there was also continuity through the entire period in the person of Nelson Aldrich, who was probably the single most powerful senator in the history of the body. Aldrich rose to power by force of personality. He held no formal position of leadership until he became chairman of the Finance Committee in 1899. Aldrich's principal co-holder of power was William B. Allison of Iowa, chairman of the Appropriations Committee from 1881 until his death in 1908, with the exception of two years when the Democrats controlled the Senate. Allison was also chairman of the Republican caucus after 1897.

Aldrich and Allison were at the center of a clique containing a number of other Republican senators. In the 1890's a group of six or eight Republican senators met regularly at the home of Senator James McMillan of Michigan for poker and politics.[12] Gradually, two principal lieutenants emerged from this group: John Spooner of Wisconsin and Orville Platt of Connecticut. "The Four" (Aldrich, Allison, Spooner, and Platt) dominated the work of the Senate from the mid-1890's until 1905, when Platt died and the remaining three began to divide on important substantive issues.[13]

Aldrich, Allison, and their group controlled the Republican party in the Senate and, through it, the entire Senate by influencing the committee assignment process, the decisions made by the caucus, the decisions made by the principal standing committees, and the scheduling decisions made by the Steering Committee.

Even during this period when the party leaders wielded great power, tension between them and the committees and individual members on substantive matters was also evident. For example, the Senate in 1899 split the appropriations function that had been centralized in the Appropriations Committee and gave some standing committees appropriating power over their subject matter fields. This decision obviously enhanced the committees' power, and was made despite the opposition of Aldrich, Allison, and their closest associates.[14]

Even during the 1890's Allison and Aldrich lost occasionally to determined opponents, such as the silver Republicans, who prevailed on some particulars of the 1897 tariff bill.[15] In the early years of the twentieth century, Aldrich lost a currency bill he favored because he got embroiled in a battle with another leading Republican over a statehood bill.[16] And when Aldrich finally left the Senate as the last of "The Four" in 1911, the system of party rule he had headed for a quarter of a century swiftly disintegrated. It had been severely strained for several years by the growing numbers of insurgents in the party.[17]

During the post-1885 period the Democrats also produced more centralized leadership than they had previously possessed. Their principal leader was Arthur Pue Gorman of Maryland, chairman of the caucus from 1889 to 1899.[18] He was floor leader, chairman of the Steering Committee, which had scheduling duties, and chairman of the Committee on Committees. His power rested on his mastery of the art of compromise within the Senate and especially within his own party. Like Aldrich and Allison he had several principal associates on whom he relied for uniting the Democrats. Unlike the Republicans, the Democratic leaders were diverse ideologically. Gorman was a minority party leader for all but two years of the 1889-1899 period. During the one Congress that his party organized the Senate, Gorman was effective in uniting the Democrats on a variety of issues, although the position taken often differed from that of the Democratic leaders in the House and the Democratic President, Grover Cleveland.

Aldrich retained substantial power in his party until his retirement in 1911; however, the formal position of Majority Leader did not emerge until he left. The Republicans appointed a different senator to be floor leader in almost every session. The chairmanship of the caucus did not correspond with the floor leadership consistently until 1913. After 1905 Aldrich retained much of his hold on the Senate, but he also lost some battles with President Theodore Roosevelt. In the Fifty-ninth Congress (1905-1907), for example, he opposed the railroad bill with all of the resources at his disposal but still was outmaneuvered by Roosevelt. He was less active in opposing the other major presidentially supported items on the legislative agenda—pure food and meat inspection—but he clearly had no use for them. Yet the Senate ignored his preferences and heeded those of the President.

In the Democratic party, power was dispersed after 1899. Gorman left the Senate in 1899, although he returned in 1903 and remained until his death in 1906. No one took his place as *the* leader of the Democrats. They too adopted the practice of appointing a different floor leader for every session. Not until 1911 did the caucus chairmanship and the floor leadership merge.

After the majority and minority leaderships became clearly identified and were formally linked to the chairmanship of the caucus (or conference, as it came to be called), the incumbents still possessed no power automatically. Active and aggressive floor leaders remained the exception rather than the rule. Institutional development of the office did not proceed much beyond clear identification of the post and the presumption both inside and outside the Senate that the holder of the post would, in fact, be the chief spokesman for his party on legislative questions. After 1945 the Republicans took some of the spotlight away from their floor leader by making the chairmanship of the conference a separate position that could not be held by the floor leader. Since World War II the Republicans have usually dispersed power among a number of leaders, including the floor leader. Occasionally, as in the Eightieth Congress (1947-1949), the man recognized as the principal Republican leader is not the floor leader, but the holder of some other post (chairman of the Policy Committee in this instance).

Table II lists the holders of the majority leadership and the minority leadership since the posts became formal and visible. Only a few of these leaders had a consistently successful impact on the operations of the Senate. Many conceived of their job as primarily that of working for orderly and efficient floor proceedings.

Among the Democrats, the post-1911 leaders that stand out as

TABLE II: SENATE FLOOR LEADERS

DEMOCRATS

Name and state	Dates of service as floor leader	Years of service	Years in Senate before election as floor leader
Thomas Martin, Va.	1911-13, 1917-19	4	16
John Kern, Ind.	1913-17	4	2
Gilbert Hitchcock, Neb.	1919	1	8
Oscar Underwood, Ala.	1919-23	3	5
Joseph Robinson, Ark.	1923-37	14	10
Alben Barkley, Ky.	1937-49	12	10
Scott Lucas, Ill.	1949-51	2	10
Ernest McFarland, Ariz.	1951-53	2	10
Lyndon Johnson, Tex.	1953-61	8	4
Michael Mansfield, Mont.	1961-	—	8
	Average (Mean)	5.6	8.3

REPUBLICANS

Name and state	Dates of service as floor leader	Years of service	Years in Senate before election as floor leader
Jacob Gallinger, N.H.	1913-18	6	22
Henry Cabot Lodge, Mass.	1919-24	6	26
Charles Curtis, Kans.	1925-29	4	16
James Watson, Ind.	1929-33	4	12
Charles McNary, Ore.	1933-43	10	16
Wallace White, Me.	1943-49	6	12
Kenneth Wherry, Neb.	1949-51	3	6
Styles Bridges, N.H.	1952-53	1	15
Robert Taft, Ohio	1953	1	14
William Knowland, Cal.	1953-59	5	8
Everett Dirksen, Ill.	1959-	—	8
	Average (Mean)	4.6	14.1

active and effective in keeping the party united and productive on legislative matters are John Kern of Indiana (1913-1917), Joseph Robinson of Arkansas (1923-1937), and Lyndon Johnson of Texas (1953-1961).

Kern's principal successes came in 1913-1915.[19] He worked closely with President Woodrow Wilson. His leadership was unobtrusive but effective. He wielded his powers of influencing committee assignments, scheduling, and chairing the caucus to unite Democrats behind the New Freedom legislative program.

Robinson's greatest successes as Majority Leader came from 1933 through 1936. He worked closely with President Franklin Roosevelt in gathering Senate Democratic support for the New Deal.[20] Robinson did not personally favor every individual New Deal bill, but his support was undeviating.

Johnson was unique in that the period of his greatest success (1955-1959) came under a President of the opposing party.[21] He worked diligently to enable every senator in his party (and some of the Republicans too) to select a rewarding role for himself that also contributed to the end that Johnson was seeking. Persuasion of many kinds characterized his operations. He realized that success depended on allowing virtually every member to maximize his own influence. Johnson's skill came in making personal maximization consistent with party success. Although the period of his leadership has some attributes of centralization, Johnson's long-term impact was to help the Senate move from decentralization to individualism. Johnson's power was largely personal, not institutional. He increased personal power specifically by dispersing choice institutional positions such as seats on the best committees and subcommittee chairmanships.

Johnson's leadership stands out more clearly because both his immediate predecessors and his successor were much less successful.[22] For example, Johnson's successor, Mike Mansfield of Montana, was unwilling to "get tough" with the rank-and-file members. He did, however, keep the scheduling powers more tightly under control than pre-Johnson Democratic Majority Leaders.[23]

Even fewer Republican floor leaders stand out as dynamic and effective. Most have not been aggressive in urging their views on the members or on standing committees. Rather, they have been willing to accept uncritically the preferences of the standing committees and work, often without much impact, for their adoption. Republican Presidents typically could not count on much aid from the floor leaders of their party. For example, Gallinger offered little aid to President Taft in the Sixty-second Congress (1911-1913). Lodge had little impact on the Sixty-seventh Congress (1921-1923) on matters other than foreign affairs and thus gave no particular help to President Harding. Curtis in the Sixty-ninth Congress (1925-1927) disagreed with President Coolidge on the main issue of the day—economic aid for farmers. Watson disagreed with Coolidge and Hoover on farm aid and with Hoover on matters of party organization and measures designed to meet the depression. Taft kept his most severe criticisms of Eisenhower's actions largely private, but opposed the President at critical points in early 1953. Knowland was much more willing to criticize the Eisenhower Administration publicly, although he tried to differentiate between his role as senator from California and his role as floor leader.[24]

Only Taft and Dirksen stand out as effective leaders of a united party. Taft apparently could develop unity in large part through his intellectual command of legislative problems.[25] It should be noted that when Taft became leader he changed his personal style by becoming more friendly with the members and spending considerably more time on the Senate floor.[26] This suggests strongly that he needed to develop personal power to supplement whatever institutional power he possessed.

Dirksen is an effective Minority Leader because he has earned the trust of the Republicans on most issues. Thus he can keep them in a united bloc and bargain for amendments, concessions, and publicity with this bloc. His power is more personal than institutional. His opportunities for enhancing his and the party's position are increased by the attitudes and actions of the Majority Leader, Mansfield.

In general, the Majority Leader and Minority Leader are expected to be the principal leaders of their party. The senators themselves, however, expect primarily that the leaders of both parties will be "Senate men" and will not automatically bow to the wishes of a President, the House or extra-congressional interests.[27] In this atmosphere of conflicting expectations, active and powerful leaders are more rare than less aggressive leaders.

The floor leaders perform all six functions of leadership. They are, or have the potential for being, the principal forces in organizing the party, scheduling business for the Senate, promoting attendance on the floor, collecting and distributing information, persuading other senators to unite with them on policy questions, and providing liaison with the White House.

The Whips [28]

Only a few years after the floor leaders became formally established, both parties elected assistant leaders or Whips. The Democrats added a Whip to their leadership in 1913, after it had become clear that the Majority Leader could use help on the floor in pressing for enactment of President Wilson's program.[29] The Republicans chose their first Whip in 1915. Table III lists all the holders of the office in both parties.

In each party six incumbent Whips have been in a position to succeed to a vacancy in the floor leadership. As Table III indicates, the three most recent Democrats to be in this position did, in fact, become floor leaders. Two out of the last three Republicans received the same promotion from their party, and the third became conference chairman.

Unlike the House Whips, the Senate Whips have never developed organizations designed to promote a systematic flow of information to and from the members. In 1965 the Democratic Whip was given four Assistant Whips, but this was merely the title bestowed on the members of the calendar committee, and signified no organizational development.[30] Furthermore, in neither party are the Whip and the floor leader automatically like-minded colleagues able to work to-

TABLE III: SENATE WHIPS

DEMOCRATS

Name and state	Dates of service as Whip	Years of service	Years in Senate before election as Whip	Advancement to floor leader [a]
J. Hamilton Lewis, Ill.	1913-19, 1933-39	12	0	no (twice)
Peter Gerry, R.I.	1919-29	10	2	no
Morris Sheppard, Tex.	1929-33	4	16	—
Sherman Minton, Ind.	1939-41	2	4	—
Lister Hill, Ala.	1941-47	6	3	—
Scott Lucas, Ill.	1947-49	2	8	yes
Francis Myers, Pa.	1949-51	2	4	—
Lyndon Johnson, Tex.	1951-53	2	2	yes
Earle Clements, Ky.	1953-57	4	2	—
Michael Mansfield, Mont.	1957-61	4	4	yes
Hubert Humphrey, Minn.	1961-65	4	12	—
Russell Long, La.	1965-69	4	16	—
Edward Kennedy, Mass.	1969-	—	6	—
	Average (mean)	4.7	6.1	

REPUBLICANS

Name and state	Dates of service as Whip	Years of service	Years in Senate before election as Whip	Advancement to floor leader [a]
J.W. Wadsworth, N.Y.	1915	0 [b]	1	—
Charles Curtis, Kans.	1915-24	10	6	yes
Wesley Jones, Wash.	1924-29	4	16	no
Simeon Fess, Ohio	1929-33	4	6	no
Felix Hebert, R.I.	1933-35	2	4	—
Kenneth Wherry, Neb. [c]	1944-49	5	1	yes
Leverett Saltonstall, Mass.	1949-57	8	4	no [d]
Everett Dirksen, Ill.	1957-59	2	6	yes
Thomas Kuchel, Cal.	1959-69	10	6	—
Hugh Scott, Pa.	1969-	—	10	—
	Average (mean)	5.0	6.0	

[a] This column indicates whether the Whip became floor leader if that position became vacant during his tenure.

[b] Wadsworth served as Whip for only one week.

[c] The Republicans appointed no Whip between 1935 and 1944.

[d] Saltonstall did, however, become chairman of the Republican Conference.

gether effectively. At times, a Whip has come from a different faction within the party than the Majority or Minority Leader. At other times, dissension has resulted from personal clashes between a Whip and a floor leader. A few Whips—Lister Hill, for example —have voluntarily given up the Whip's job while still remaining in the Senate because they did not feel that the position was worth their time. Apparently possessing the title gave them little additional satisfaction.

The Whips can help the floor leaders perform the six basic functions of party leadership, although most Whips have not been consistently important in doing so. Their aid is peripheral, not central, to the impact of the floor leaders.[31] Only a few have developed into major influences in the party, usually through their performance of the persuasion function.

The Party Conferences

Since the earliest days of the Senate, the members of the parties have met together in caucuses or conferences. In the mid-1840's the caucuses acquired power over committee assignments.[32] In theory, the caucuses developed binding power over their members on substantive legislative questions, but in practice, parties in the Senate have chosen not to use a formally binding caucus. Early in the twentieth century both parties substituted the name "conference" for "caucus," a formal recognition of the lack of binding power. In spite of this change, however, the psychological pressure generated by a conference may produce a binding effect.

The party caucuses became especially important on substantive and scheduling questions in the period during and after the Civil War.[33] But this new importance was not secure and not fully accepted by the members until the mid-1880's. During the war itself the Republican caucus debated and adopted substantive policies, which were then expected to engage the full support of all Republican senators. After the war and the passage of the basic Reconstruction measures, caucus control relaxed substantially, although the caucus continued to involve itself in scheduling decisions, sometimes directly and sometimes through a committee on the order of business. Substantive matters continued to be discussed but formal votes did not occur often. The party remained split on many substantive questions before the mid-1880's.

From the mid-1880's until about 1911 the Republican caucus met on most major legislative questions in order to seek unity. Impressive unity was achieved between 1889 and 1900 on roll-call votes.[34] On the major bills, such as the tariff bill in 1897, the caucus made the basic substantive decisions, replacing, in effect, the standing committee.[35] The impact of the caucus is summarized by the leading student of this period: "The Republican caucus was not binding, and yet its decisions commanded obedience for party leadership was capable of enforcing discipline. Senators could no longer act with impunity unless they were willing to forego favorable committee posts and control of the chamber proceedings."[36]

Before 1885 the Democratic caucus possessed little power. Even after the rise of Gorman to power in the party the Democrats remained more divided than the Republicans on substantive questions, and their leadership apparatus did not lend itself to effective discipline. Finally, in 1903, the Democrats decided to make their caucus decisions binding. "Most Senate Democrats, despite sporadic protestations over the unequal distribution of authority, were dissatisfied with the lack of party harmony. Whatever ambivalence they felt toward more powerful colleagues, the great majority keenly desired to bring stability to the organization. Since the chairmen could not accomplish the task alone, they ruled all caucus decisions binding. . . . [W]ith only two dissenting votes, the Democrats resolved that the vote of two-thirds of the party compelled the obedience of every member in the Senate."[37] There is no evidence, however, that the Democrats ever used the binding caucus. In 1913, when they specifically proposed to hold one, the objections were so strong that the project was dropped.[38] In 1933 the Democrats again adopted a binding rule for the caucus by a vote of 50 to 3. This rule required only a majority vote and was limited to "any measure recommended by the President . . ." But there is no evidence that this form of the binding caucus was used either; the Democrats' action was reflective of the economic crisis and a demonstration of their complete faith in Franklin Roosevelt. In that Congress, however, nonbinding conferences were used to good effect.[39] Since that time the Democrats have met only occasionally on substantive matters and there has been no further serious attempt to institute a binding caucus.

The Republicans formally replaced the title "caucus" with "conference" in early 1913.[40] They have never come close to adopting a binding rule, but they have continued to use their conference for the discussion of legislative matters more frequently than have the Democrats.

At present, the chief function of the Democratic conference is to organize the party. It also plays a limited role in collecting and distributing information. The Republican conference performs these two functions and also, because it meets more often and discusses legislative questions, involves itself in persuasion.

Steering and Policy Committees

Shortly after the Civil War the majority party in the Senate—usually the Republicans—began to recognize the need for a more orderly scheduling of business for floor action.[41] For a few years the Republican caucus attempted to make scheduling decisions itself, but this proved to be both clumsy and controversial. In 1874 the Republicans appointed a committee of the caucus to prepare a schedule. This procedure proved more successful and was repeated in succeeding years until the mid-1880's, when a formal Steering Committee, appointed by the caucus chairman, emerged to make scheduling decisions. This committee was firmly under the control of Aldrich and his closest associates.

This body, renamed the Policy Committee in 1947, has remained continuously in existence for the Republicans. At present, because the Republicans are in the minority, the Policy Committee cannot make scheduling decisions. Instead, it is more concerned with discussing policy positions that the Republicans should take, although it rarely takes such positions by formal action.

The Democratic counterpart of the Republican Steering Committee was slower to emerge, largely because the Democrats almost never controlled the Senate. But in the first post-Civil War Congress (1879-1881) in which they organized the Senate and thus had responsibility for scheduling business, they quickly imitated the Republicans and appointed a committee on the order of business called the Steering Committee. The committee reappeared on those infrequent occasions when the Democrats controlled the Senate. It soon merged with the Committee on Committees, although it retained its original name.

In 1947 the Democrats created a Policy Committee that reassumed the scheduling functions of the old Steering Committee without assuming any policy role. Thus, in the present Democratic Senate party the Steering Committee is the committee on committees and the Policy Committee aids the floor leader in scheduling. The floor leader chairs the present Policy Committee and appoints all of its members.

Committees on Committees [42]

The parties did not directly control committee assignments until 1846, when the party caucuses performed the task of ratifying assignments suggested by the party leaders. This system lasted only three years before the pre-Civil War multiplication of parties made it unworkable. During the war, the Republicans used a committee on committees (a committee of the caucus) to make all assignments, even for the few remaining Democrats.

By the beginning of the postwar period the Republicans had

established a Committee on Committees that was appointed by the caucus chairman every two years. The membership of the committee continually changed. Party loyalty was now a major consideration in its operations: the committee was free to use a variety of criteria in its appointments because the demands of seniority were not, as yet, completely supreme. Seniority was a strong force, but not until a decade or two after the war did it become virtually the only criterion for determining rank on committees and chairmanships. The party could, for example, remove Charles Sumner as chairman of the Foreign Relations Committee in 1871 because of his opposition to President Grant's Santo Domingo policy, despite his loud protests that the honored traditions of seniority were being violated.

Another instance of growing party discipline occurred in December, 1872, following the bolt of the Liberal Republicans from Grant to Greeley in the presidential campaign of that year. Roscoe Conkling's faction of the party began regularly to control the principal committee assignments through domination of the Committee on Committees. This control solidified in the hands of the Aldrich-Allison group. The chairman of the caucus, always loyal to the Aldrich-Allison group, retained the power to appoint the Committee on Committees. Seniority determined rank on a committee, but since the Committee on Committees determined initial committee assignments, the composition of committees was controlled by the party leader.

Gradually, during the twentieth century, the Republican Committee on Committees ceased to have independent power. The Republicans began to make seniority in the Senate the absolute criterion for initial assignment to committees as well as for promotion in rank on committees. Members would, however, sometimes change committees at the leaders' request so that reliable and deserving members could be distributed among the important committees.[43]

Before the mid- or late-1870's the Democrats did not use a formally constituted committee on committees. There were few Democrats in the Senate until then and they could not hope to have much influence on the work of the committees in any case. But when election results put them within striking distance of control and then, in 1879, actually gave them control, the Democrats too formed a Committee on Committees, named and chaired by the caucus chairman. It has come to be bound by seniority for promotions, but has never been completely bound in terms of original assignments or shifts in assignments. Loyalty to party or at least to the prevailing ideology of the committee on committees has often helped determine initial assignments.

Party Development in the Senate

A similar three-stage development of the parties in both the House and the Senate took place beginning in about the mid-1870's. First, the party leaders in both houses centralized available resources and power in their hands. Second, both bodies became relatively institutionalized, particularly by the professionalization of the congressional career and the hardening of seniority as the overwhelmingly important criterion for committee rank. Third, the parties in both houses developed bureaucratic characteristics, chiefly in the form of a number of elected party leaders and leadership committees.

This process took different forms in the two houses, however. In the House the process was largely sequential, with one stage leading directly into and helping to cause the succeeding stage.[44] In the Senate the process was largely simultaneous, with all three stages feeding on each other, partially caused and partially causal. Table IV summarizes the developmental process in both houses.

In the House, the Speaker (regardless of party) led in centralizing power. Two additional central leaders (Majority Leader and Whip) emerged shortly thereafter as lieutenants to the Speaker. Following that, a professionalization of the House career led to demands from

TABLE IV: PARTY DEVELOPMENT IN THE HOUSE AND THE SENATE

STAGE OF DEVELOPMENT	HOUSE	SENATE
Centralization of power	1875-95	1885-95
Institutionalization		
Professionalization of career	1890-1910	1875-95
Hardening of seniority	1911-25	1885-95
Bureaucratization		
Central leadership positions	1897-1900	1911-15
Party committees and organizations	1919-present	1885-95

the members that the Speaker's power be limited so that they could count on orderly and nonarbitrary advancement. Then the central party leaders, in order to recoup some of the power lost by the hardening of seniority and in order to combat divisive forces within the parties, helped the parties bureaucratize themselves by means of such devices as whip organizations and steering and policy committees.

The centralization of power in the Senate in the hands of party leaders took place under Aldrich, Allison, and their associates in the Republican party and under Gorman and his associates in the Democratic party. This centralization was rapid and occurred largely in the late 1880's and early 1890's.

The professionalization of the Senate career took place concurrently with the centralization of power. Incumbent senators began winning elections with greater ease, in part because they were in many cases gaining effective control of state political machines that, barring a party overturn, could guarantee their reelection in the state legislatures.[45] After the Civil War the Senate became a highly attractive place in which to make a political career. It rapidly became apparent that the Senate dominated national political decisions, and it remained dominant for the last few decades of the nineteenth century. Senators had, until roughly the late 1870's and

1880's, readily resigned their seats for business opportunities, governorships, judgeships, and other pursuits. Now once a man was in the Senate he tended to remain there unless he could leave to be President or a member of the cabinet. Figure I reflects the changing pattern in terms of mean years of service for all senators at the beginning of each Senate.

The figure shows that the most dramatic and sustained period of increasing service occurred between 1875 and 1893. In most of the pre-1875 Senates the average senator had served for around four years. In most of the post-1893 Senates the average senator had served for about twice as long. There have, of course, been fluctuations—most notably in this century the dip connected with the influx of new Democrats before and during the Wilsonian era and the fairly steady increase in the last two decades to the present peak. The continuing increase in the late 1880's and early 1890's is particularly impressive when it is remembered that six new states joined the union in those few years, adding twelve new senators who were, of necessity, quite junior in 1893.

Seniority as the criterion for committee advancement (although not initial appointment) hardened at the same time that senators were becoming professionals. Table V summarizes the use or nonuse of seniority as the criterion for advancement to committee chairmanships or ranking minority memberships among the Republicans from 1865 to 1899. 1877 marks a clear turning point: between 1865 and 1877 seniority was rarely used as the criterion for advancement to the top position on a committee; after 1877 seniority was almost never violated.

Among the Democrats a similar development took place, although data on ranking minority members during the period of complete Republican dominance from 1861 to 1877 is spotty. Some important committees during this period had no Democratic members and others had only one. The Democrats were so few in number and so impotent that the concept of "ranking minority member" meant little in terms of actual power.

FIGURE I

AVERAGE YEARS OF SERVICE – ALL SENATORS

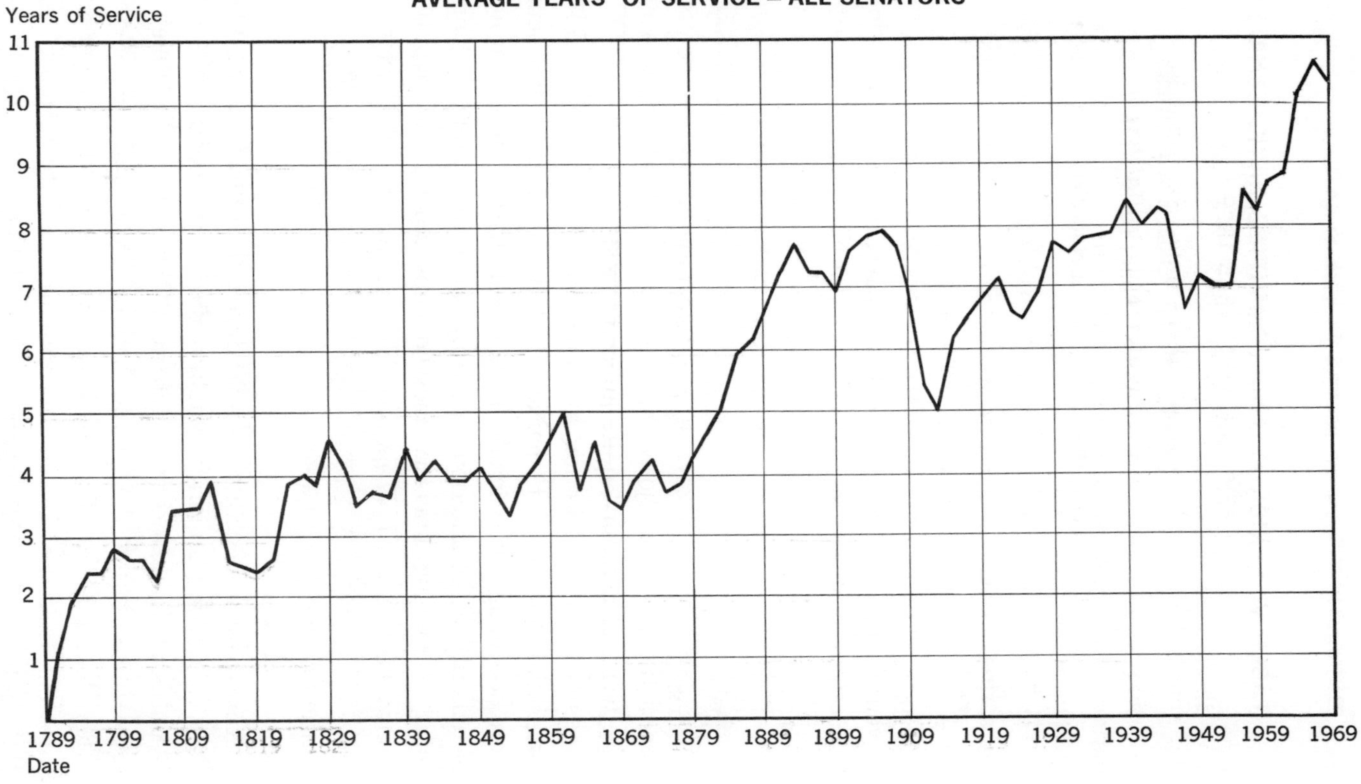

TABLE V: SENIORITY AND COMMITTEE RANK, SENATE REPUBLICANS, 1865-1899

YEAR	CHANGES IN TOP REPUBLICAN POSITIONS ON TEN STANDING COMMITTEES [a]		
	Seniority used	Seniority violated	Unclear
1865	3	0	0
1867	0	2	1
1869	0	1	0
1871	0	3	1
1873	1	4	0
1875	0	1	1
1877	5	0	2
1879	2	0	1
1881	5	0	1
1883	2	1 [b]	0
1885	0	0	1
1887	3	1	0
1889	1	0	0
1891	2	0	0
1893	2	0	0
1895	3	0	0
1897	3	0	0
1899	1	0	0

[a] The ten committees were chosen because of their importance. They are the Committees on Foreign Relations, Finance, Appropriations, Commerce, Military Affairs and the Militia, Naval Affairs, the Judiciary, Post Offices and Post Roads, Public Lands, and Agriculture.

[b] This violation of seniority involved the removal of a third-party member from a chairmanship.

Data for Democrats before the Civil War suggest that seniority was becoming the rule before the Democratic party virtually disappeared from the Senate in 1861. Data after 1879 indicate that when the Democrats again had substantial weight in the Senate seniority was only rarely violated. Table VI summarizes these data.

The reason for this sudden emergence of seniority as virtually the sole criterion for committee advancement lies principally in the

TABLE VI: SENIORITY AND COMMITTEE RANK, SENATE DEMOCRATS, 1847-59; 1881-99

YEAR	CHANGES IN TOP DEMOCRATIC POSITIONS ON TEN STANDING COMMITTEES [a]		
	Seniority used	Seniority violated	Unclear
1847	1	4	0
1849	5	2	0
1851	1	3	1
1853	2	0	0
1855	3	0	0
1857	3	1	0
1859	1	0	0
—	—	—	—
1881	6	0	0
1883	1	1	0
1885	4	0	0
1887	1	0	0
1889	1	0	0
1891	1	0	0
1893	2	0	0
1895	3	1	0
1897	4	0	0
1899	4	1	0

[a] The committees are the same as those used for Table V.

size of the majority possessed by the Republicans. As Figure II makes clear, the Republicans had no sizable Democratic contingent with which to contend until after 1875. From then on the Democrats consistently comprised close to half the Senate until almost the end of the century, although they were able to capture a majority only twice.

Before 1877 the ruling Republican clique could afford to alienate some of the Republican senators and, because of the party's complete domination in numbers, still count on legislative success. After 1877 this was impossible: the Republican leaders needed the sup-

FIGURE II

PARTY STRENGTH IN THE SENATE, 1861-1905

Note: Third-party members are omitted

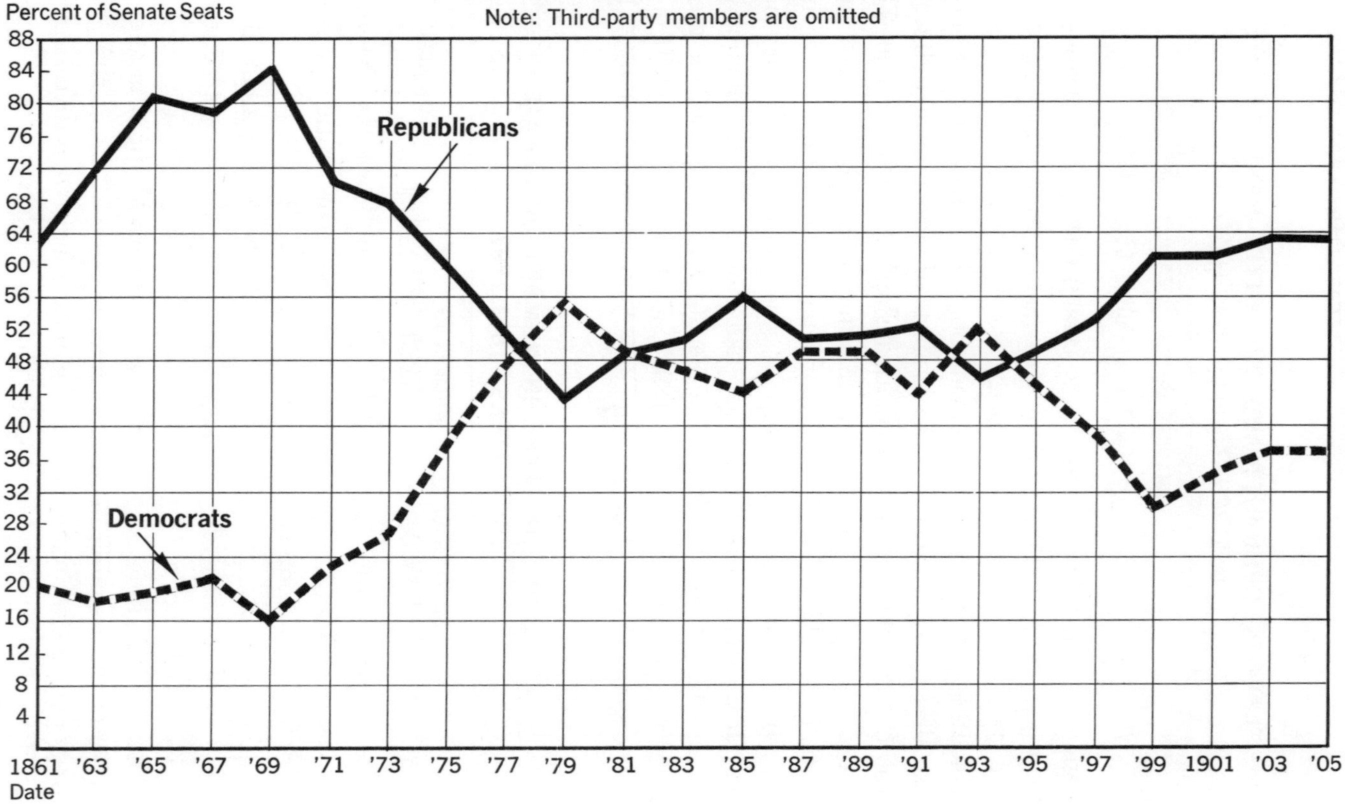

port of all Republicans. One way to work for this support was to acquiesce to an automatic and impartial rule for committee advancement. The leaders of the party thus helped institute this limit on their own power.

Simultaneously, however, the leaders enhanced their power by urging the expansion of numbers of committees. This increase gave them greater flexibility in initial assignments. Men whom they did not trust could be relegated to the less important committees, of which there were now a greater number. The expansion in number also allowed the leaders to make requests of individual Republicans who became eligible for two chairmanships at the same time. The leaders were often able to influence a man whom they trusted only partially to take the less important chairmanship, thus preserving the more important chairmanship for a person over whom they had greater control and in whom they had more faith. The figures on the number of committees in the Senate reveal a period of great growth in the 1880's and early 1890's, as shown in Table VII.

The greatest period of growth came between 1881 and 1885, by

TABLE VII: INCREASE IN NUMBER OF SENATE COMMITTEES, 1861-1897

YEAR	NUMBER OF STANDING COMMITTEES	NUMBER OF SELECT COMMITTEES	TOTAL	PERCENT CHANGE
1861	22	3	25	—
1865	23	0	23	− 8
1869	26	1	27	+17
1873	28	3	31	+15
1877	28	3	31	0
1881	30	4	34	+10
1885	39	8	47	+38
1889	42	11	53	+13
1893	46	13	59	+11
1897	49	10	59	0

which time it had become clear that seniority was likely to dominate selection of committee chairmen for a long time.

Once the Democrats had elected enough senators to influence substantive outcomes, they, too, wished to avoid the risk of alienating any of their own members by choosing between them in decisions on committee advancement.

The nature of bureaucratization has differed in the two houses. The first formal party organs to appear in the Senate were committees: the committees on committees and the steering committees. In the House, individual leadership positions appeared first. The Senate party committees handled two functions that had become extremely important in a Senate that was dominating the national legislative process: scheduling and making standing committee assignments. The personalities of the leading senators—Aldrich, Allison and Gorman—were such that they did not need formal leadership positions to control their parties. Allison and Gorman eventually became caucus chairmen, but this position was not essential to their control. Aldrich never held an official position other than that of chairman of the Finance Committee, which he did not achieve until 1899.

After these dynamic leaders left the Senate, however, both parties soon made the floor leadership and an assistant floor leadership (the Whip) formal positions visible to all. The Republicans were torn by dissension between their insurgents and their regulars in the early years of the twentieth century, and they responded to this threat by creating formal positions. The Democrats could see after the 1910 election that they were very likely to control the Senate shortly. They gained that control, along with the control of the White House, in the 1912 election. They were then faced with the necessity of uniting the party behind a large and popular legislative program being urged on them by the President. They, too, responded by making formal leaders responsible for keeping the majority united and oriented toward legislative achievement. Bureaucratization essentially ceased for the Democrats with this development.

The Republicans have continued to bureaucratize, most notably by creating a Policy Committee in 1947.

In general, then, two factors pushed senators of both parties to organize themselves so as to have a consistent and important impact on legislative matters. First, by the mid-1870's the Democrats became strong enough to pose a constant threat to Republican control of the Senate. Second, the lack of party control led to chaotic conditions in the late 1860's, 1870's and early 1880's. This frustrated the senators in their attempts to be legislatively effective.

The key to understanding the differences between the developmental sequences in the House and Senate is the use of seniority as the principal criterion for committee assignments. In the House this did not emerge as the sole criterion for serving on committees and advancement to chairmanships until *after* the leaders (principally the Speaker) had centralized power in their hands. This meant that the Speaker retained arbitrary power over committee assignments. When greatly increased numbers of House members began a career of House service they resented this arbitrary power and seized on seniority as a way of limiting it.

In the Senate, on the other hand, seniority as the principal criterion for committee advancement had hardened *before* the leaders centralized power in their hands. Thus the members of the Senate, who also began in increasing numbers to make careers in the Senate, were already protected against arbitrary action by the leaders on the all-important matter of progression in committee status. They could, therefore, afford to cooperate with the leaders in positive legislative activity. The career senator who emerged in the late nineteenth century was, according to the historian of the period, "Ready to follow while eagerly awaiting the opportunity to lead . . ."[46]

Seniority had hardened in the Senate earlier than in the House largely because of the absence of alternatives. The Speaker of the House had always been a central and powerful figure and early acquired the power to make committee assignments. The Senate, of course, had no equivalent of the Speaker, and each Senate tended to decide for itself how to assign its members to committees. No committees on committees emerged until after the Civil War. No single leader emerged as the logical appointing authority. The Senate had a great deal of difficulty making assignments during much of the period immediately before the war. Thus seniority emerged as the only practical way of solving the problem of status on the committees, although it did not solve the problem of initial assignment.

The small size of the Senate accounts in large part for the attenuation of the bureaucratization process. The necessities of coverage are not as great in a body of 100 as they are in a body of 435. Thus the Senate leaders had less reason to push for additional organization than the House leaders. Also, even after the emergence of powerful leaders in the 1880's, senators retained a number of publics other than leaders to which they could appeal for approval and thus gain satisfaction. They had no pressing reason to demand organizational developments as a means of dispersing power.

Notes

[1] See Ralph K. Huitt, "The Morse Committee Assignment Controversy: A Study in Senate Norms," *American Political Science Review*, Vol. 51 (June 1957), pp. 313-329, on instances of this description in 1925 and 1953.

[2] See George Goodwin, "The Seniority System in Congress," *American Political Science Review*, Vol. 53 (June 1959), pp. 412-436, on a 1953 Democratic modification and a 1959 Republican modification.

[3] This brief review of the development of Senate committees is based on George Lee Robinson, "The Development of the Senate Committee System" (Ph.D. dissertation, New York University, 1954).

[4] For this interesting debate see *Congressional Globe*, 35th Cong., 1st sess. (1857-1858), Pt. 1, pp. 38-42.

[5] James S. Young, *The Washington Community, 1800-1828* (Columbia University Press, 1966), p. 95.

[6] *Ibid.*, footnote on pp. 104-105.

[7] *Ibid.*, p. 147.

[8] George H. Haynes, *The Senate of the United States: Its History and Practice* (Houghton Mifflin, 1938), pp. 285-288.

[9] David J. Rothman, *Politics and Power in the United States Senate, 1869-*

1901 (Harvard University Press, 1966), p. 15. See chapter 1 generally on this point.

[10] On the 1869-1885 period for the Republicans see Rothman, *Politics and Power*, pp. 15-35.

[11] Woodrow Wilson, *Congressional Government* (Meridian, 1956), pp. 146-147.

[12] Rothman, *Politics and Power*, p. 45; Dorothy G. Fowler, *John Coit Spooner: Defender of Presidents* (University Publishers, 1961), pp. 137-138.

[13] Nathaniel W. Stephenson, *Nelson W. Aldrich: A Leader in American Politics* (Scribner's, 1930), pp. 132-137; Fowler, *Spooner*, pp. 200-202, 329-338. On 1885-1901 generally, see Rothman, *Politics and Power*, pp. 43-61. On the specific workings of the Aldrich leadership in the Fifty-ninth Congress (1905-1907) see Randall B. Ripley, *Majority Party Leadership in Congress* (Little, Brown, 1969), chapter 2.

[14] Rothman, *Politics and Power*, pp. 66-67.

[15] Stephenson, *Aldrich*, pp. 142-144.

[16] *Ibid.*, pp. 210-211.

[17] See for example, Shelby M. Cullom, *Fifty Years of Public Service: Personal Recollections of Shelby M. Cullom* (McClurg, 1911), pp. 419-425. For what happened to the Republicans in the Senate immediately after Aldrich left, see Ripley, *Majority Party*, chapter 5.

[18] On Gorman's leadership see Rothman, *Politics and Power*, pp. 61-69; and John R. Lambert, *Arthur Pue Gorman* (Louisiana State University Press, 1953).

[19] See Claude G. Bowers, *The Life of John Worth Kern* (Hollenback, 1918); and Ripley, *Majority Party*, chapter 3.

[20] See Ripley, *Majority Party*, chapter 3; and Nevin E. Neal, "A Biography of Joseph T. Robinson" (Ph.D. thesis, University of Oklahoma, 1958).

[21] See Ralph K. Huitt, "Democratic Party Leadership in the Senate," *American Political Science Review*, Vol. 55 (June 1961), pp. 333-344; Rowland Evans and Robert Novak, *Lyndon B. Johnson: The Exercise of Power* (New American Library, 1966); and Ripley, *Majority Party*, chapter 5.

[22] On Johnson's predecessors see, for example, William S. White, *Citadel* (Harper, 1957), p. 106.

[23] See Ripley, *Majority Party*, chapter 2.

[24] On Gallinger, Lodge, Curtis, Taft, and Knowland see Ripley, *Majority Party*, chapters 4 and 5. On Watson see James E. Watson, *As I Knew Them* (Bobbs-Merrill, 1936), chapter 9.

[25] See White, *Citadel*, p. 105.

[26] See Richard Rovere, *Affairs of State: The Eisenhower Years* (Farrar, Straus, and Cudahy, 1956), pp. 103-112.

[27] White, *Citadel*, p. 96.

[28] See *Congressional Quarterly Weekly Report*, September 25, 1964, pp. 2251-2252.

[29] *New York Times*, May 29, 1913. *Congressional Quarterly* incorrectly dates the creation of the Democratic Whip's job in 1915.

[30] See the column by Evans and Novak in the *Washington Post*, January 19, 1966.

[31] The whip organizations are much more important to the leaders in the House. See Randall B. Ripley, "The Party Whip Organizations in the United States House of Representatives," *American Political Science Review*, Vol. 58 (September 1964), pp. 561-576.

[32] Rothman, *Politics and Power*, pp. 13-14.

[33] See *ibid.*, chapters 1 and 2.

[34] See *ibid.*, p. 89.

[35] Fowler, *Spooner*, p. 205.

[36] Rothman, *Politics and Power*, p. 60.

[37] *Ibid.*, p. 68.

[38] See Ripley, *Majority Party*, chapter 3.

[39] *Ibid.*

[40] Haynes, *Senate*, p. 475.

[41] On the development of the Republican Steering Committee before 1900 see Rothman, *Politics and Power*, pp. 17, 18, 30, 48-49, 58-59.

[42] On the pre-Civil War developments, see Haynes, *Senate*, pp. 285-289. On the developments from the Civil War to 1900 see Rothman, *Politics and Power*, pp. 16, 17, 26, 28, 36, 49-51, 63.

[43] For an example of this phenomenon see Shelby M. Cullom, *Fifty Years*, p. 344.

[44] For a full statement of this argument on the House, see Randall B. Ripley, *Party Leaders in the House of Representatives* (Brookings, 1967), chapter 2.

[45] Rothman, *Politics and Power*, chapter 6.

[46] *Ibid.*, p. 136.

Chapter 3: **Power in the Post-World War II Senate: From Decentralization to Individualism**

The distribution of legislative power in the Senate has changed since the end of World War II. The point of this chapter is that between 1945 and 1968 the Senate has transformed itself from a body in which principal legislative power resided in the chairmen and, to a lesser extent, the ranking minority members of the full standing committees into a body in which significant legislative power is spread among virtually all senators of both parties. This also means that the Senate has changed from a body in which most important legislative decisions were dominated by conservative southern Democrats into a body in which many important legislative decisions are not dominated by conservative southern Democrats.

Commentators who knew well the Senate of the late 1940's and

53

early and middle 1950's concluded that a conservative oligarchy, variously identified as the Club or Establishment, ruled the Senate.[1] They asserted that the rule of the oligarchy is perpetuated in part by the continuing emergence of "Senate men" who possess certain personal traits acceptable to the ruling oligarchs. These traits include tolerance for others, courteousness, prudence, and a willingness to help others, to work hard, to compromise, and to keep one's word.[2] The "Senate man" is devoted to certain practices or "folkways" of the Senate: a period of apprenticeship for new members and legislative specialization, for example.[3] Those supporting the Club argument assert that men who do not conform to the model do not wield as much influence or power in the Senate as those who do. The important posts are reserved for members of the Club and the important decisions, legislative and institutional, are made by them.

Those who discern a Club or Establishment in the Senate do not necessarily agree on the identity of all of its members. But they do agree that the Club in both parties has both a geographical and an ideological bias: it is dominated by southern Democrats and midwestern Republicans who are dedicated to blocking most liberal legislation, whether sponsored by a Democratic or Republican President.

Those who contest the validity of the Club analysis cite the lack of agreement on its membership.[4] They point out that senators who violate the folkways and do not possess all of the requisite personal traits—men such as Hubert Humphrey, for example—have been identified as members of the Club. They also point out that even the complete, self-acknowledged "outsider" can have substantial power, both because of the committee structure of the Senate and because of the great bargaining weight automatically available to each one of the hundred senators. They argue that members of the so-called Establishment—southern and a few western Democrats—often provide the deciding votes in favor of liberal legislation.

It would seem that both sides in this dispute are partially correct, but for different periods of time.

THE DEMOCRATS AND INSTITUTIONAL POWER

Two critical events in 1946 shaped the post-World War II Senate and gave the southern Democrats a dominant institutional position that only now is beginning to diminish.[5] The first of these events was the passage of the Legislative Reorganization Act, which necessitated a reshuffling of committee assignments when the Eightieth Congress met in early 1947. The second was the election of November 1946. Once these two events had established the southerners in a strong position in the committee hierarchy of the Senate then what they needed to develop dominance was continued reelection and good health and the continued preference of the voters for a Democratic majority.

After the 1946 election the Democrats found themselves with 45 Senate seats instead of 56. The regional composition of the party had swung south:[6]

	SOUTHERN SEATS	WESTERN STATES	NORTHERN STATES
1946	22	19	15
1947	22	13	10

This change had both immediate and long-run effects on the seniority structure of the party. Immediately, the southerners occupied a stronger position at the highest levels of seniority. For example, in 1946, only two of the nine most senior Democrats in the Senate were from southern states. Five of the nine were loyal supporters of Roosevelt's and Truman's domestic programs. After the 1946 election four of the nine most senior Democrats were from southern states and only three of the nine were loyal supporters of New Deal and Fair Deal legislation.

Death, as well as defeat, caused the average seniority of all Democrats from both the South and outside the South to decline for a few years after 1946. But the southerners rapidly began to increase their seniority again while further electoral misfortunes continued to plague northerners and westerners. Mean seniority figures (in years) by region reflect this situation:

	1945	1949	1953
Southern Democrats	9.7	8.5	9.2
Northern and western Democrats	8.3	7.6	7.0

The skill of the conservative southerners in perpetuating the strongest possible institutional position for themselves while, at the same time, keeping the chances of revolt by liberals at a minimum, can be suggested by looking at committee reorganization in 1947. During 1945 and 1946 a Joint Committee on the Organization of Congress worked on a number of proposals for modernizing Congress. One of the keys to reform was the standing committee system in both houses. In the Senate, thirty-three standing committees existed in 1946. The Legislative Reorganization Act, signed by the President in August 1946, reduced this number to fifteen and reduced the number of seats on each committee. At the beginning of the next Congress, in January 1947, the Senate put the revised committee structure into operation. Now there were only 86 seats on the six most sought-after committees (Appropriations, Armed Services, Finance, Foreign Relations, Interstate and Foreign Commerce, and Judiciary) instead of 143.[7] Democrats in the Seventy-ninth Congress had held 86 seats on these committees; now they had only 39. The Republicans were more fortunate: their representation on these committees shrunk from 57 seats to 47 seats.

During 1945 and 1946, as the Joint Committee began to work on the specifics of committee consolidation, a great deal of bargaining took place. All thirty-three Democratic chairmen (and the thirty-three ranking Republican members) had an especially heavy stake in reorganization. Even the chairman of an inconsequential committee was entitled to certain perquisites, and few chairmen were happy at the prospect of losing these perquisites and becoming just another committee member. Thus a senator who was to lose a chairmanship presumably should get something for it: either assignment to a choice committee on which he had not previously served or retention of a choice committee on which he already had some service.

The Democratic problems were compounded by the election results in November 1946, which decreed that the next Senate would be Republican. Thus the Democrats would have only ranking minority memberships to pass out, not chairmanships, and they would have fewer seats on the choice committees. But the bargains made before the election would still have to be kept. Those Democrats who were slated to be chairmen of the reorganized committees would now have to be content with being number one on the minority side.

The southern Democrats lost more top positions than they retained, but they retained the most important positions. Of the twelve committee chairmen in the Seventy-ninth Congress who returned to the Eightieth Congress and retained their top ranking positions on the Democratic side of the successor committee, only four were southerners. They were, however, first ranking on three of the most important committees: Appropriations, Finance, and Foreign Relations.

Twelve men who chaired committees in the Seventy-ninth Congress and who returned to the Eightieth Congress lost their top ranking positions on the successor committee. Some left the successor committee altogether. Some also lost assignments on other choice committees, not always because of the new Republican-Democratic ratio after the 1946 elections. Some of these men apparently agreed to give up choice seats to men with less seniority as part of the general reassignment bargain.

Two of the twelve men who lost committee chairmanships and did not retain the ranking minority position were Alben Barkley and Scott Lucas who were, respectively, floor leader and Whip. Obviously, their leadership duties were important and time-consuming, and so their changed committee positions cannot be considered a "loss." Of the other ten who "lost" in the committee shuffle, six were southerners. Table VIII summarizes what happened to the ten "losers" in the 1946-1947 shuffle.

Several generalizations can be made from this table. First, the committees that these men lost were not very important by themselves: only Civil Service and Education and Labor had much legislative responsibility prior to the Reorganization Act. In both cases, western Democrats lost these places to more senior western Democrats. Only two men with more seniority than their successors as first ranking lost (apparently voluntarily) their committee assignments. These were both southerners: Lister Hill of Alabama and Richard Russell of Georgia. But they both retained much more important committee assignments: Hill as number four on Armed Services and number five on Labor and Public Welfare and Russell as number five on Appropriations and number two on Armed Services. Hill also lost a place on Foreign Relations, but only because of the changed committee ratio in 1947.

The men who lost the most were the six who not only lost a chairmanship but who also lost a seat on Foreign Relations or Military Affairs (which merged with Naval Affairs to become Armed Services) to a Democrat junior to them on the committee, not just because of the 1946 election results. Of these six, only two were from southern states: Claude Pepper of Florida and Tom Stewart of Tennessee. Pepper was clearly a southern "maverick"—he was one of the most liberal Democrats in the Senate. Stewart was quite junior by southern standards and apparently expendable. The other four "losers" who suffered the most were three liberal westerners and a liberal New Englander. In short, five supporters of President Truman lost most heavily in the committee reorganization, and only one man reasonably loyal to the southern conservative group was among the heaviest losers.

The non-southern "losers" were, however, mollified by the committee assignments they did receive. They lost more than they retained or gained, but they still had enough to prevent serious thoughts of protest. Downey retained Public Lands and got an

LEGISLATIVE REORGANIZATION ACT OF 1946

NAME, STATE	YEARS OF SERVICE IN 1946	CHAIRMAN, 1946	SUCCESSOR COMMITTEE	1947 COMMITTEE ASSIGNMENTS	RANK	ALSO LOST[a]
Downey, Cal.	7	Civil Service	Civil Service	Public Lands Public Works[b]	4 4	Military Affairs
Ellender, La.	9	Claims	Judiciary	Agriculture and Forestry Labor and Public Welfare	2 4	
Murray, Mont.	11	Education and Labor	Labor and Public Welfare	Labor and Public Welfare Public Lands	2 3	Foreign Relations Military Affairs
Hill, Ala.	8	Expend. in Exec. Depts.	Expend. in Exec. Depts.	Armed Services Labor and Public Welfare	4 5	
Russell, Ga.	13	Immigration	Judiciary	Appropriations Armed Services	5 2	
O'Mahoney, Wyo.	12	Indian Affairs	Public Lands	Appropriations Public Lands	8 2	Military Affairs
Stewart, Tenn.	7	Interoceanic Canals	Armed Services	Agriculture and Forestry Interstate and Foreign Commerce	4 2	Military Affairs
Pepper, Fla.	9	Patents	Judiciary	Agriculture and Forestry[b] Labor and Public Welfare	6 3	Foreign Relations
Green, R.I.	9	Privileges and Elections	Rules	Appropriations Rules	9 2	Foreign Relations
Byrd, Va.	13	Rules	Rules	Armed Services Finance	3 4	

[a] These assignments were lost to men of lesser seniority on the committee, not just because of the changed party ratio in the Senate.
[b] New assignment in 1947. All other assignments represent continuations of previous assignments.

additional assignment to Public Works—both important committees for California. Murray, perhaps the heaviest single loser in the reorganization, retained high ranking positions on Labor and Public Welfare and Public Lands, the latter of great importance to Montana. O'Mahoney retained a junior position on Appropriations and second position on Public Lands, important for Wyoming. Green retained a junior position on Appropriations.

Thus, those in the strongest positions during reorganization understood both how to perpetuate the interests of their own group and how to reduce the chances of violent objection.

Using their seniority position and their political skills to highest advantage, the southerners, especially the conservatively oriented ones, came, within a few years after World War II, to dominate the standing committees of the Senate. Growing regional overrepresentation in the late 1940's and early 1950's can be documented, and some commentators have specifically attempted to document the overrepresentation of the southern Democrats on committees.[8] But these documentations either give no indication of the degree of overrepresentation involved or they lack the time perspective that would facilitate determination of trends.

Table IX presents data that show the pattern of southern Democratic overrepresentation in critical institutional positions. This overrepresentation decreased from a high level before and during World War II for the decade after the war. From the mid-1950's until the mid-1960's it grew in the areas of committee chairmanships, the top three seats on all standing committees, and the top three seats on the four most important committees.[9]

The two areas in which southern overrepresentation has been decreasing since the mid-1950's are in subcommittee chairmanships and in all seats on the four most important committees. The spread of subcommittee chairmanships and junior seats on choice committees had the effect of keeping dissent and revolt against a southern-dominated committee system at a minimum.

The latest figures, for 1968, show that southern overrepresentation

TABLE IX: SOUTHERN DEMOCRATIC REPRESENTATION ON SENATE COMMITTEES AND SUBCOMMITTEES, 1941-1968 [a]

CONGRESS (YEAR)	All Democratic senators	Committee chairmen [b]	PERCENT OF SOUTHERNERS AMONG:			
			Three highest ranking Democrats on all committees [c]	All Democrats on four choice committees [d]	Three highest ranking Democrats on four choice committees [d]	Subcommittee chairmen [e]
77th (1941)	33	62	48	36	67	
79th (1945)	39	50	44	35	50	
81st (1949)	41	40	42	54	67	
83rd (1953)	47	47	56	56	67	
85th (1957)	45	53	44	58	58	45
87th (1961)	34	56	48	46	67	41
89th (1965)	29	62	52	43	83	35
90th (1968)	30	56	46	37	67	31

[a] The South is defined as the eleven states of the Confederacy.

[b] This column applies to ranking minority members in the Eighty-third Congress, when the Republicans organized the Senate. This column indicates the sixteen most important standing committees in the Seventy-seventh and Seventy-ninth Congresses (Agriculture and Forestry, Appropriations, Banking and Currency, Commerce, District of Columbia, Education and Labor, Finance, Foreign Relations, Interstate Commerce, Irrigation and Reclamation, Judiciary, Manufactures, Military Affairs, Naval Affairs, Public Lands and Surveys, and Rules), and all standing committees thereafter.

[c] This column includes the sixteen most important standing committees in the Seventy-seventh and Seventy-ninth Congresses and all standing committees thereafter.

[d] The four choice committees are Appropriations, Armed Services, Finance, and Foreign Relations. Military Affairs was used instead of Armed Services in the Seventy-seventh and Seventy-ninth Congresses.

[e] Data on subcommittees are difficult to obtain before 1955. A few special subcommittees of little importance are omitted from this tabulation.

TABLE X: IDEOLOGICAL BIAS OF DEMOCRATIC CONTINGENTS ON SIX SENATE COMMITTEES, 1947-1967

COMMITTEE	RELATION OF COMMITTEE CONTINGENT TO ALL DEMOCRATS ON BASIS OF 20 INDEX SCORES [a]	
	More conservative	More liberal
Appropriations	18	2
Armed Services	16	3
Commerce	10	9
Finance	19	0
Foreign Relations	6	11
Judiciary	18	2

[a] The two figures for each committee do not add to 20 in all cases because some mean committee scores are the same as the mean score for all Democrats.

on all of the various measures used is declining. The institutional base of southern power seems to be eroding, although slowly.

Not only have the southerners as a regional grouping been dominant on the most important committees and in the most important positions on all committees, but the *conservative* southerners and their allies and ideological comrades from other regions have dominated most of the six committees on which most senators want to serve: Appropriations, Armed Services, Commerce, Finance, Foreign Relations, and Judiciary.

In order to determine ideological biases in the Democratic contingents on these committees, comparisons were made for all Congresses from 1947 (Eightieth) through 1967 (Ninetieth) between the mean scores of the Democrats on each of the six committees on various *Congressional Quarterly* indices and the mean score for all Democrats in those Congresses. Table X reports summary findings. Comparative party unity index scores, presidential support scores under Kennedy and Johnson, and federal role support scores were interpreted for evidence of liberal or conservative bias in the composition of the Democratic membership of these six committees.

The data support the proposition that during this period the conservative Democrats were dominant on Finance, Appropriations, Judiciary, and Armed Services. The Commerce Committee was not consistently under the control of any ideological group, and the liberals tended to control the Foreign Relations Committee.

When these scores are examined individually, there is evidence that a gradual liberalization of the Democratic contingents on these six committees is taking place. For example, Table XI compares the number of Democrats more liberal or more conservative than the average Democratic senator on the six committees in the Eighty-fifth Congress (1957-1958) and in the Ninetieth Congress (1967-1968). The score used for making judgments in the former case is the Economy Opposition Score and the score used for the latter is the Larger Federal Role Support Score.

TABLE XI: IDEOLOGICAL BIAS OF DEMOCRATIC CONTINGENTS ON SIX SENATE COMMITTEES IN THE EIGHTY-FIFTH AND THE NINETIETH CONGRESSES

COMMITTEE	EIGHTY-FIFTH CONGRESS		NINETIETH CONGRESS	
	Liberals	Conservatives	Liberals	Conservatives
Appropriations	5	7	8	9
Armed Services	4	4	7	5
Commerce	3	5	8	4
Finance	3	5	4	7
Foreign Relations	6	2	8	4
Judiciary	2	6	7	4
Total	23 (44%)	29 (56%)	42 (56%)	33 (44%)

These figures suggest a broader pattern: conservative Democrats are hanging on to their dominance of a few key institutional positions, in this case the Finance Committee, but are seeing their former control of some positions, in this case the Commerce Committee and Judiciary Committee, disappear. In other cases, such as the Appropriations Committee and the Armed Services Committee, the changes are incrementally in the liberal direction. The picture emerges of a slowly dissolving institutional power base for conservative Democrats.

Southern representation on the Democratic Steering Committee (the committee on committees) helps explain southern dominance on the most important committees from 1951 to 1965. Table XII summarizes this representation for twelve Congresses. From 1951 to 1965 southern representation on the Steering Committee was consistently just short of half of the committee. This southern strength, coupled with the electoral system in the southern states that has usually returned the same man for term after term, has led naturally to southern dominance of the Democratic side of most of the important committees. Generally, the southerners entered the Senate at a younger age than the other Democrats. This gave them an added advantage in accruing seniority: they could outlive

TABLE XII: SOUTHERN REPRESENTATION ON DEMOCRATIC STEERING COMMITTEE (COMMITTEE ON COMMITTEES), 1945-1967

CONGRESS (YEAR)	NUMBER ON COMMITTEE	NUMBER OF SOUTHERNERS ON COMMITTEE	PERCENT OF SOUTHERNERS ON COMMITTEE	PERCENT OF ALL DEMOCRATIC SENATORS FROM SOUTH
79th (1945)	11	3	27	39
80th (1947)	14	4	29	49
81st (1949)	11	3	27	41
82nd (1951)	13	6	46	45
83rd (1953)	15	7	47	47
84th (1955)	14	6	43	46
85th (1957)	15	7	47	45
86th (1959)	15	7	47	34
87th (1961)	15	7	47	34
88th (1963)	15	7	47	31
89th (1965)	17	7	41	29
90th (1967)	17	5	29	30

other Democrats more often than not. The figures for 1967, however, suggest that here, too, the institutional base for southern power is dwindling.

The southern Democrats had general, although not universal, success in keeping the formal top leadership offices of the party under their control. Nine men held the position of floor leader or Whip between 1947 and 1968. Two men held the position of secretary of the caucus from 1961 to 1968.[10] These eleven men constituted the central leadership of the Democratic party in the Senate for these twenty-two years. Three were from southern states, three were from border states, three were from western states, and only two were from the heavily populated states north of the Ohio River and east of the Mississippi River. Only one of the eleven, Hubert Humphrey, had or acquired a national reputation as a leader of the liberal wing of the party. Most of the men were balancers, trying to find a way for the party to stick together, either in inactivity or in activity upon which agreement could be reached. A few were in the conservative wing of the party.

When contests between moderates or conservatives and liberals took place (only three out of a possible fourteen times) the moderate or conservative always won. In 1951 the conference elected Ernest McFarland of Arizona, a moderate dominated by the southerners, as Majority Leader over Joseph O'Mahoney of Wyoming, a staunch Fair Dealer.[11] In 1965, Russell Long of Louisiana won a three-way race for Whip over his more consistently liberal opponents, John Pastore of Rhode Island and Mike Monroney of Oklahoma.[12] In 1967, conservative Robert Byrd of West Virginia defeated liberal Joseph Clark of Pennsylvania for the post of Secretary of the Conference.

Part of the reason for the present slow erosion of southern conservative institutional power is numbers: only 19 of a party of 64 in the Ninetieth Congress were southerners and a number of those were liberals. Liberal Democrats who were assigned to junior positions in 1959 and succeeding years are now, through the inexorable process of seniority and the boost given them by the Goldwater candidacy in 1964, succeeding to more important positions.

In addition to changing personnel, several other factors have led to a dispersion of institutional power. The "Johnson rule" for committee assignments—that all Democrats should have one good assignment before any Democrat has more than one—began spreading influential positions to more junior senators soon after its adoption in 1953.[13]

Furthermore, throughout the late 1950's and early 1960's the number of subcommittees increased. In part, this increase reflected the skill of the southerners in keeping incipient revolt suppressed. It also reflected a real dispersion of power, occasioned in part by the growing workload in the Senate. Figures for 1957, 1961, 1965, and 1968 show the number of subcommittees (and thus chairmanships) increasing, but southern representation declining, as shown in Table XIII.

TABLE XIII: PROPORTION OF SOUTHERNERS SERVING AS SUBCOMMITTEE CHAIRMEN, 1957-1968

CONGRESS (YEAR)	NUMBER OF SUBCOMMITTEE CHAIRMEN	NUMBER OF SOUTHERN CHAIRMEN	PERCENT OF SOUTHERN CHAIRMEN
85th (1957)	86	39	45
87th (1961)	95	39	41
89th (1965)	98	34	35
90th (1968)	103	32	31

Most northern and western Democrats have subcommittee chairmanships. These bestow both tangible perquisites (including, in some instances, control over staff appointments) and increased influence on legislation on the incumbents. Not all subcommittees are equally powerful, however, and senior southerners can in many cases retain the most important subcommittee chairmanships for themselves and their allies. Thus, again, the erosion of southern institutional power is gradual.

In the Eighty-ninth Congress (1965-1966), for example, only sixteen Democrats (out of sixty-eight) failed to attain either committee or subcommittee chairmanships. Table XIV lists these senators.

Only two of the twenty southern Democrats had no subcommittee chairmanship. One was a freshman and so had no reason to expect a chairmanship and another had a high ranking position on Finance, which has no subcommittees, and a junior position on Foreign Relations. Neither, then, had reason to feel aggrieved.

Of the fourteen northern and western Democrats without chairmanships, four were freshmen. Five of the remaining ten had assignments on Appropriations, Armed Services, or Finance in which they could take consolation. Thus, five non-southern, nonfreshman Democrats held neither a subcommittee chairmanship nor a seat on one of the most important four committees in the Senate. These senators—one midwesterner and four from the Far West—had some consolation. Three of the far-westerners were on Interior and Insular Affairs, which handles matters vital to their region. One of these had been a subcommittee chairman on the Interior Committee in the Eighty-eighth Congress. A senior westerner had waived seniority in order to give him this chairmanship in a year in which he faced what looked like a close election fight. After he was reelected, the more senior westerner reclaimed the subcommittee. The fourth westerner had made evident her lack of interest in running for another term in the Senate.

THE DEMOCRATS AND PERSONAL POWER

The personal skill of the southerners in manipulating the Senate has been widely publicized by those writing about the Senate of the 1940's and 1950's.[14] They seemed to control critical organizational and legislative decisions, but often subtly enough to avoid

TABLE XIV: DEMOCRATS AT THE BEGINNING OF THE EIGHTY-NINTH CONGRESS (1965) WHO WERE NEITHER COMMITTEE NOR SUBCOMMITTEE CHAIRMEN

NAME, STATE	YEARS OF SERVICE IN 1965	COMMITTEE ASSIGNMENTS	RANK
Bartlett, Alas.	6	Appropriations	16
		Commerce	5
Bass, Tenn.	0	Agriculture and Forestry	9
		Commerce	12
Brewster, Md.	2	Armed Services	12
		Commerce	10
Burdick, N.D.	5	Interior and Insular Affairs	7
		Judiciary	10
		Post Office and Civil Service	8
Harris, Okla.	0	Government Operations	7
		Public Works	12
Hartke, Ind.	6	Commerce	6
		Finance	9
		Post Office and Civil Service	7
Inouye, Hawaii	2	Armed Services	10
		Public Works	9
Kennedy, N.Y.	0	District of Columbia	4
		Government Operations	8
		Labor and Public Welfare	11
McCarthy, Minn.	6	Agriculture and Forestry	7
		Finance	8
McGovern, S.D.	2	Agriculture and Forestry	8
		Interior and Insular Affairs	9
Mondale, Minn.	0	Aeronautical and Space Sciences	10
		Banking and Currency	10
Montoya, N.M.	0	Agriculture and Forestry	10
		Government Operations	10
		Public Works	11
Moss, Utah	6	Interior and Insular Affairs	6
		Public Works	6
Nelson, Wisc.	2	Interior and Insular Affairs	10
		Labor and Public Welfare	10
Neuberger, Ore.	4	Banking and Currency	8
		Commerce	11
Smathers, Fla.	14	Finance	3
		Foreign Relations	11

angering many of those against whom they worked. The graciousness and professional competence of the southerners helped assuage the liberals' pain. They magnified the power that came to them through seniority by their skilled and judicious *use* of seniority. They understood the dynamics of power and their own relation to changing circumstances in the Senate and in the country at large. They accommodated when necessary, for they knew that intransigence rapidly causes the loss of influence. They never were able to win on everything in which they had an interest; but they possessed the most advantageous bargaining positions on matters in which their interests were deepest.

But by the mid-1960's a new situation had emerged in which a number of moderately senior and very junior Democrats, virtually all liberals, had begun to develop significant impact on important legislative matters.[15] They began to make impressive records of their own in their subcommittees. At the same time, several of the senior conservative oligarchs were removed by defeat, death, or retirement. Several more are in bad health or may face electoral problems.

By the mid-1960's virtually all Democrats were content with their lot in the Senate specifically because they perceived that they could be effective legislatively on some matters that were or had become important to them. In subsequent chapters of this volume these perceptions are explored.

THE REPUBLICANS AND INSTITUTIONAL POWER

The principal role of most of the Republicans in the Senate during the postwar years, at least until Everett Dirksen became Minority Leader in 1959, was to support the conservatively-oriented Democrats and their leaders. With the exception of Robert Taft, Republicans were not the leaders in the coalition with the southern Democrats.

Within the Republican party the conservatives (most notably

TABLE XV: MIDWESTERN REPUBLICAN REPRESENTATION ON SENATE COMMITTEES AND SUBCOMMITTEES, 1941-1968 [a]

CONGRESS (YEAR)	PERCENT OF MIDWESTERNERS AMONG:					
	All Republican senators	Ranking members on committees [b]	Three highest ranking Republicans on all committees [c]	All Republicans on four choice committees [d]	Three highest ranking Republicans on four choice committees [d]	Ranking members on subcommittees [e]
77th (1941)	53	56	46	48	58	
79th (1945)	51	50	58	60	58	
81st (1949)	43	47	49	44	58	
83rd (1953)	40	53	53	39	33	
85th (1957)	38	47	44	41	25	51
87th (1961)	34	50	42	39	33	45
89th (1965)	28	31	30	38	42	35
90th (1968)	29	37	33	39	50	39

[a] The Midwest is defined to include Ohio, Indiana, Illinois, Michigan, Wisconsin, Minnesota, Iowa, North Dakota, South Dakota, Nebraska and Kansas.

[b] This column applies to chairmen in the Eighty-third Congress, when the Republicans organized the Senate. This column includes the sixteen most important standing committees in the Seventy-seventh and Seventy-ninth Congresses (Agriculture and Forestry, Appropriations, Banking and Currency, Commerce, District of Columbia, Education and Labor, Finance, Foreign Relations, Interstate Commerce, Irrigation and Reclamation, Judiciary, Manufactures, Military Affairs, Naval Affairs, Public Lands and Surveys, and Rules,) and all standing committees thereafter.

[c] This column includes the sixteen most important standing committees in the Seventy-seventh and Seventy-ninth Congresses and all standing committees thereafter.

[d] The four choice committees are Appropriations, Armed Services, Finance, and Foreign Relations. Military Affairs was used instead of Armed Services in the Seventy-seventh and Seventy-ninth Congresses.

[e] Data on subcommittees are difficult to obtain before 1955. A few special subcommittees of little importance are omitted from this tabulation.

from the Midwest) have not consistently controlled the top committee and leadership positions.[16] But, of central importance to
understanding the situation in the Senate in the 1950's, the conservatives and midwesterners tended to be overrepresented during
that period. At present, liberal Republicans from outside the Midwest hold just as many positions of importance as the conservative
midwesterners.

Commentators on the Senate who have indicated that the southerners are exceptionally powerful in the Democratic party also
usually indicate that the midwesterners are exceptionally powerful
in the Republican party.[17]

In order to test this proposition, some of the same kinds of data
that were collected on the southern Democrats were also collected
on the position of midwestern Republicans within their party. Table
XV summarizes the position of midwesterners in relation to the
committee assignments open to Republicans.

The Republican pattern is just the reverse of the Democratic
pattern. Among the Democrats, the southerners were most overrepresented at the beginning of the 1941-1965 period and again
at the end of it. By 1968 their overrepresentation had begun to
decline. In the middle of the period the southerners had about the
representation that their numbers entitled them to. Among the
Republicans, as the table shows, the midwesterners were most overrepresented in the middle of the 1941-1965 period. In 1968 their
position was somewhat stronger again.

The Republicans have not kept their contingents on the most
important standing committees in the hands of the conservatives.
Data on various party and ideological indices for the years between
1947 and 1967 suggest that only the Finance Committee contingent
was regularly controlled by conservatives. Appropriations Committee Republicans have tended to be more liberal than most Republicans, especially in the most recent years. The other committees
have tended to vacillate between liberal and conservative weighting.
Table XVI summarizes these data.

TABLE XVI: IDEOLOGICAL BIAS OF REPUBLICAN CONTINGENTS ON SIX SENATE COMMITTEES, 1947-1967

COMMITTEE	RELATION OF COMMITTEE CONTINGENT TO ALL REPUBLICANS ON BASIS OF 20 INDEX SCORES [a]	
	More conservative	More liberal
Appropriations	4	13
Armed Services	8	10
Commerce	10	8
Finance	19	1
Foreign Relations	8	12
Judiciary	10	10

[a] The two figures for each committee do not add up to 20 in all cases because some mean committee scores are the same as the mean score for all Republicans.

The primary reason for the lack of party control by the conservative Republicans, except in the case of the Finance Committee, is that not only committee changes but also initial assignments were made on the basis of seniority. Thus the Republican committee on committees had only very limited opportunities to "stack" committees regionally or ideologically. Occasionally, however, senior Republicans claimed a vacancy for ideological reasons. For example, Taft in 1947 took the Labor and Public Welfare Committee chairmanship, rather than that of Finance, to prevent a more liberal member from obtaining it. Dirksen in 1963 took a seat on Finance for the same reason.

When the Republicans had to make the bargains that led to the reshuffling of committee assignments prompted by the Legislative Reorganization Act of 1946, they had a somewhat easier task than the Democrats. Fewer members were likely to be affected adversely since, in 1946, a few of the most senior Republicans held three or four first-ranking positions each.[18] Presumably they could keep their major ranking positions if the party continued in the minority in 1947; they would not mind giving up the minor ranking positions. If the party became a majority in 1947, each ranking member would become chairman on one committee, and the other chairmanships would be available to other Republicans.

When the party actually became the majority in the Senate in 1947, it did not have to deprive many men of chairmanships. The four Republicans who lost the top ranking place on a committee did not have to give up their other choice assignments. All of the four who were displaced retained assignments on either Finance or Appropriations. Table XVII lists these men and summarizes their committee positions. Only Senator Reed was senior to the men who became chairmen of two committees on which he had previously served. But he retained high ranking positions on Appropriations and Interstate and Foreign Commerce.[19] Three of the four senators displaced from chairmanships were midwestern Republicans and all were succeeded by midwesterners.

Of the ten Republicans who returned to the Eightieth Congress and retained their top ranking committee positions, six were midwesterners.

In short, in 1946-1947, the Republicans, both because of the relatively small number of men holding ranking positions before reorganization and because of the electoral victory in 1946, were able to redistribute powerful committee posts without seriously impairing the standing of any Republican who had gained a powerful position before the reorganization.

Since 1947 most Republican leaders have been clearly identified with the conservative element in the party. Three moderately liberal members have also held one of the top positions, but none has become floor leader. Twelve different senators held the positions of floor leader, Whip, chairman of the conference, and chairman of the Policy Committee between 1947 and 1968. Of these, five were from the Midwest, three from the Far West, and four from New England. Of the seventeen changes in the top leadership positions between 1947 and 1968, only four were contested. The conservative candidate won three of the four contests in the conference.[20]

TABLE XVII: REPUBLICANS WHO LOST FIRST POSITION ON A COMMITTEE BECAUSE OF THE LEGISLATIVE REORGANIZATION ACT OF 1946

NAME, STATE	YEARS OF SERVICE IN 1946	RANKING MEMBER, 1946	SUCCESSOR COMMITTEE	1947 COMMITTEE ASSIGNMENTS	RANK
Bushfield, S.D.	3	Interoceanic Canals	Armed Services	Agriculture and Forestry	3
				Finance	5
Ball, Minn.	5	Immigration	Judiciary	Appropriations	5
				Labor and Public Welfare	3
				District of Columbia [a]	3
Brewster, Me.	5	Library	Rules	Finance	4
				Interstate and Foreign Commerce	4
Reed, Kans.	7	Mines and Mining	Public Lands	Appropriations	4
		Post Office	Civil Service	Interstate and Foreign Commerce	3

[a] New assignment in 1947. All other assignments represent continuations of previous assignments.

These data support the conclusion that institutional power is also widely dispersed in the Republican party at present. For example, by 1965 power was so widespread that no Republican, including freshmen, was without a ranking minority position on at least one committee or subcommittee. This situation resulted in part from a combination of small numbers of men and large numbers of sub-committees. It had the added effect of making life tolerable in what must seem to Republicans to be perpetual minority status. The midwestern conservative Republicans were not as skillful in retaining power for themselves as the southern Democrats, a fact which suggests that a regional group in a minority party loses the incentive to retain power after a number of years in the minority. Unless ideological purity is important to a number of the minority leaders, shared power makes for a more pleasant existence when most of the power rests in the hands of the majority party anyway.

In addition, the Republicans modified their absolute rule of seniority for committee assignments in 1959 informally and in 1965 formally and gave more chance to junior Republicans to be impor-tant legislatively.

THE REPUBLICANS AND PERSONAL POWER

When Everett Dirksen became Minority Leader in 1959 he grad-ually began to disavow ideological purity as a goal of his leadership. His predecessors had, with varying degrees of success, insisted on it. In the pre-Dirksen climate it was difficult for junior Republicans to develop personal power. Dirksen's style fosters the development of such power.

In 1949, for example, when Kenneth Wherry of Nebraska was Minority Leader, the predominantly conservative midwesterners were overrepresented on all of the important committees. Wherry insisted on extremely conservative principles as the only true Re-publican principles. William Knowland, the floor leader from 1953 through 1958, was torn between being a good soldier for Eisenhower and being a dedicated conservative. Either way he tended to expect the Republicans to follow his lead. Dirksen was not much concerned with ideological purity and from 1961 to 1969 did not have a President of his own party. On a few major matters, such as civil rights, a nuclear test-ban treaty, and a loan for the United Nations, he was concerned that he produce as much Republican support for his position as possible, in these cases positions also espoused by Democratic Presidents. But in the normal working of the Senate he is usually content to leave every individual Republican free to develop influence by pursuing his own course of action in his own way.[21]

In this climate a number of junior Republicans began to exercise their new-found ability to have legislative impact.[22] The Republicans' perceptions of legislative effectiveness are explored in subsequent chapters.

SUMMARY

The shifting patterns of power distribution in the post-World War II Senate are best understood if two types of power are analyzed: institutional power and personal power. If institutional power alone were studied, the data would support the conclusion that only now is the hold of the southern Democrats on the Senate beginning to weaken; and it was at its peak during the mid-1960's. Yet this same period of the mid-1960's, especially 1965, was a period of great liberal legislative activity that met with success in many fields. Thus it is suggested that a study of institutional power is necessary, but used alone it cannot logically explain some outcomes. Institutional power is not enough to explain the southern hold on the Senate in the 1950's; after all, the southerners never did control *all* of the important positions. They needed allies, and the techniques they used to identify and win those allies involve personal power. Institutional power is not enough to explain the liberal output of the Senate in the mid-1960's either. Liberal non-southern senators of both parties had begun to develop personal power that allowed them to neutralize and even overcome much of the institutional advantage that the conservative southerners still possessed.

In the late 1960's analyses of both types of power point the same way: important institutional positions are being dispersed ever more widely and there are few obstacles to any senator of either party who has the requisite personal skills to develop legislative power and chooses to use those skills.

Notes

1 The classic Club and Establishment arguments are presented in William S. White, *Citadel* (Harper, 1957), and Joseph S. Clark and Other Senators, *The Senate Establishment* (Hill and Wang, 1963). The idea is still persuasive to some. See Clayton Fritchey, "Who Belongs to the Senate's Inner Club?", *Harper's* (May 1967), pp. 104-110.

2 These two sentences are based on the summary in Ralph K. Huitt, "The Outsider in the Senate," *American Political Science Review*, Vol. 55 (September 1961), pp. 566-567. Huitt, of course, was disputing the validity of some of the argument.

3 See Donald R. Matthews, *U.S. Senators and Their World* (University of North Carolina Press, 1960), pp. 92-102. Woodrow Wilson was less specific than Matthews on the content of Senate "folkways," but he described the same phenomenon in general language: "If a new Senator knock about too loosely amidst the free spaces of the rules of that august body, he will assuredly have some of his biggest corners knocked off and his angularities thus made smoother; if he stick fast amongst the dignified courtesies and punctilious observances of the upper chamber, he will, if he stick long enough, finally wear down to such a size, by jostling, as to attain some motion more or less satisfactory." Woodrow Wilson, *Congressional Government* (Meridian, 1956), pp. 145-146.

4 See Nelson W. Polsby, *Congress and the Presidency* (Prentice-Hall, 1964), chapter 3. See also the speech by Majority Leader Mike Mansfield in 1963 rebutting the charges of Senator Clark and others that the "establishment" controls committee assignments and legislative results, *Congressional Record*, Vol. 109, Pt. 3, 88th Cong., 1st sess. (1963), pp. 2918-2922.

5 There is no implication here that all southern Democrats think or vote alike. But as a group they were clearly more conservative than other regional groups of Democrats. For material on the complexities of differentiating southern Democrats from other Democrats see H. Douglas Price, "Are Southern Democrats Different? An Application of Scale Analysis to Senate Voting Patterns," in Nelson W. Polsby, Robert A. Dentler, and Paul A. Smith, eds., *Politics and Social Life* (Houghton Mifflin, 1963), pp. 740-756.

6 For Democratic senators the South is defined as the eleven states of the Con-

federacy. The West includes all states West of the Mississippi River except Arkansas, Louisiana, and Texas. The North includes the rest.

[7] These committees were designated as "most sought after" because from 1947 to 1966 they were the only committees that consistently gained more members than they lost. This means that senators were eager to obtain seats on them and were usually not willing to leave them voluntarily. For the figures on 1947-1957 see Matthews, *U.S. Senators*, pp. 148-150. For the figures on 1957-1966 see Stephen Horn, *Unused Power: A Study of the Senate Committee on Appropriations* (forthcoming), chapter 2.

[8] See, for example, George Goodwin, "The Seniority System in Congress," *American Political Science Review*, Vol. 53 (June 1959), pp. 412-436, Table 3 and related text; and Clark, *The Senate Establishment*, pp. 105-106.

[9] The four most important committees (Appropriations, Armed Services, Finance, and Foreign Relations) are, like the six most sought after committees that have been referred to previously, chosen by the senators themselves. For example, when the Republican senators changed their committee assignment procedure in 1965 they specifically labeled these four as the most important to them.

[10] The position of Secretary of the Conference has existed since at least 1907. Until 1961, however, the Secretary had no importance inside the party. George Smathers of Florida, elected in 1961, began to attend White House meetings with the other leaders. His successor, Robert Byrd of West Virginia, became important within the party in a wide variety of ways within a few months after his election as Secretary in January 1967. See the *Washington Post*, October 4, 1967, for a fine analysis of this development.

[11] The same year Lyndon Johnson, then moderately conservative, became Whip. The only other name put forward seriously was John Sparkman of Alabama, who chose not to run. Sparkman was a much more loyal supporter of the Truman program than Johnson. See Rowland Evans and Robert Novak, *Lyndon B. Johnson: The Exercise of Power* (New American Library, 1966), p. 43. Evans and Novak mistakenly assert that McFarland was unopposed. In fact, the contest between McFarland and O'Mahoney was decided by a 30 to 19 vote in the Democratic conference. A few days later the liberal Democrats complained they had been treated unfairly in committee assignments. See *New York Times*, Jan. 3, 1951, and Jan. 6, 1951.

[12] Long himself was defeated for Whip in early 1969 by the more liberal Edward Kennedy of Massachusetts.

[13] Johnson had a consuming desire to unite the party and prevent intraparty strife such as had occurred during the preceding two years. With the cooperation of Senator Russell he persuaded a number of Senior Democrats, including some southerners, that a modification of the use of seniority for committee assignments was for the benefit of all. See Evans and Novak, *Johnson*, pp. 63-64; and *New York Times*, Feb. 15, 1953.

[14] See, for example, White, *Citadel*; and Howard E. Shuman, "Senate Rules and the Civil Rights Bill: A Case Study," *American Political Science Review*, Vol. 51 (December 1957), pp. 955-975.

[15] For persuasive journalistic accounts of this change in both parties see Dan

Cordtz, "The Senate Revolution," *Wall Street Journal*, Aug. 6, 1965; Tom Wicker, "Winds of Change in the Senate," *New York Times Magazine*, Sept. 12, 1965; Meg Greenfield, "Uhuru Comes to the Senate," *Reporter*, Sept. 23, 1965; and Robert C. Albright, "Senate Youngsters Asserting Selves as Never Before," *Washington Post*, January 15, 1968.

Nelson Polsby, writing about the Senate in *Congress and the Presidency*, p. 45, concludes, referring to both parties, that "We can think of the internal politics of the Senate not as a small group of powerful men surrounded by everyone else, but as a group which divides labor and power—unequally to be sure, but still significantly—among almost all its members."

Even Senator Clark agreed that "the old Senate establishment is gone. Democracy is now pretty much the rule in the Senate." *Congressional Record*, Vol. 111, Pt. 17, 89th Cong., 1st sess. (1965), p. 23495.

[16] No suggestion that all midwestern Republicans think and vote conservatively and can be set off clearly from the rest of the party on these grounds is intended. A few midwesterners have been non-conservatives and some non-midwesterners have been among the conservative leaders. Ideological differences are not as closely related to region in the Republican party as in the Democratic party. But the conservative center of gravity among Republicans is in the midwesterners.

[17] See, for example, Goodwin, "The Seniority System," Table 3 and related text. The Midwest includes Ohio, Indiana, Michigan, Wisconsin, Illinois, Minnesota, Iowa, North Dakota, South Dakota, Nebraska, and Kansas.

[18] Senator Arthur Capper of Kansas was ranking Republican on Agriculture and Forestry; Claims; District of Columbia; and Foreign Relations in 1946. Senator Charles Tobey of New Hampshire was ranking Republican on Audit and Control of Expenses in the Senate; Banking and Currency; and Naval Affairs. Senator Arthur Vandenberg of Michigan was ranking Republican on Commerce; Rules; and Territories and Insular Affairs. Senator Robert LaFollette, Jr., of Wisconsin, held the top minority party position on Education and Labor; Finance; Indian Affairs; and Manufactures.

[19] Reed led an unsuccessful attempt to prevent the holders of party leadership positions from also holding committee chairmanships. His failure to advance in committee standing was punishment for his efforts. See *New York Times*, Dec. 27, 1946, and Jan. 2, 1947. Taft clearly dominated the party during the period of reorganization. See *New York Times*, Dec. 31, 1946, and Jan. 3, 1947.

[20] In early 1969 two leadership contests were decided by the Republican conference. The conference selected the more liberal candidate for Whip and the more conservative candidate for chairman of the Policy Committee.

[21] On Wherry see Truman, *The Congressional Party*, pp. 106-108. On Knowland see Ripley, *Majority Party Leadership*, chapter 4. On Dirksen see Meg Greenfield, "Everett Dirksen's Newest Role," *Reporter*, Jan. 16, 1964; and Murray Kempton, "Dirksen Delivers the Souls," *New Republic*, May 2, 1964.

[22] The material cited in footnote 15, preceding, gives a number of examples of such impact.

Dispersion of Power in the Contemporary Senate

Chapter 4: **Party Leadership**

Background material on the present Senate has now been presented and general suggestions about its shape have been offered. The remainder of this volume explores the present Senate in depth. This analysis relies on data collected in fourteen round table discussions with senators and staff members held in 1965, individual interviews with other senators and staff members, and a variety of scholarly and journalistic sources for reports on Senate events.[1]

The structure of legislative life in the present Senate does not permit domination by party leaders, committee chairman, or senior senators. It also protects the Senate, at least psychologically, from domination by the executive branch or by the House of Representatives. Every senator, however new, may develop a specialization in which his opinion will be regarded as authoritative by the whole Senate. This chapter analyzes the degree of influence over the Senate's legislative actions exercised by contemporary party leaders. Even in an individualistic situation the leaders retain some importance.

IDENTITY OF PARTY LEADERS

The Democratic View

Democratic senators at present face a situation of diffuse, shifting, and unstable leadership. The formally elected Majority Leader is only *part* of the party's leadership.

The Democratic senators regard the main task of the formal leaders (Majority Leader, Whip, and Secretary of the Democratic Conference) as important, but quite limited. According to one senator, they "meet with the President once a week and sit down, therefore, with the Administration and Cabinet members who may be there. They bring back the viewpoint of the Executive and communicate what the Administration wants." But what the Administration wants constitutes only a small part of what the Senate does legislatively. According to a senior Democrat, "About 90 percent of the congressional activities are routine. They are things the President doesn't take a strong interest in. Ten percent would probably be of very special interest to the Administration, and that is where you have communication through the formal leadership."

In addition to the formal leaders, the senators most likely to be considered as part of the leadership are committee and subcommittee chairmen. Almost all Democratic senators are eligible to become part of the constantly shifting leadership group. This eligibility has expanded in the last few years because of the generational changes in the Senate (new men with different attitudes acquiring some seniority and the staunchest leaders of the "Old Guard" dead, retired, defeated, or ill and tired of combat) and because of the Majority Leader's permissive attitudes toward individual legislative activity.[2] A skillful Democratic senator is now in a position to make the most of the opportunities that come his way. Senator Edmund Muskie of Maine, for example, in 1963 became the chairman of two important subcommittees only four years after entering the Senate. Rapidly he used these positions to become *the* Senate authority on intergovernmental relations and air and water pollution. The central leaders, the chairmen of the parent committees, lobbyists, and bureaucrats all acknowledge his primacy.[3]

Democratic senators at the round tables discussed the widespread availability of leadership roles:

A: A senator will be part of the leadership one day and will be a wild-eyed opponent the next day. I remember Albert Gore [of Tennessee] was the white hope on the Medicare bill when it passed last year. He carried the ball on that bill. Yet he will fight the Administration on tax matters and on many items.

B: There are two factors. Either one becomes a committee chairman or moves up fairly close; or one develops expertise. Some men interest themselves in and work on and know a lot about leadership when that is the subject of conversation. Then they may fade right out again when they move on to something else. I think the leadership is a shifting group.

C: I think you had a good example of this last week with Wayne Morse [of Oregon] on the Education Bill. You would have to say in all fairness that 90 percent of the time he would not be considered a part of the leadership, and yet here he was carrying the ball, and certainly at the moment was a very important part of the leadership in shepherding this bill through.

A: You can say generally that leadership comes from subcommittee structure, because when the ball was passed to Wayne, as chairman of that subcommittee, he forgot all about the role he likes to play as maverick, and became part of the leadership for the moment. He was interested in getting a majority vote and lobbied people to get it.

In addition to subject-matter experts, other types of Democrats are also leaders. First, there are men so generally revered in the Senate that they can speak with authority and lead other senators on substantive matters that come from a variety of committees. Second, there are men for whom junior senators feel special respect.

The junior men are willing to take advice from some senators on a wide range of matters—including which committees to apply for —although they do not always follow it on substantive legislative matters. Ideological differences in no way undermined the respect one freshman senator felt for a senior:

I would ask him, for instance, what type of committee I should try to get on, or what I should do when I first get to the Senate. There are certain senators that everyone universally respects. At least, all of the older senators respect him. You sense it, you feel it. I will give you a strong example: Senator [John] Stennis. I just sense that everyone in the Senate respects Senator Stennis. He is not a committee chairman, he is from Mississippi, but as far as I am concerned, he is a fine senator, and he is the type of man I would go to to seek advice. And he tries to help you. He takes an interest in the new senator. He invites me to breakfast once a week.

No Democratic senator is excluded permanently from this shifting leadership group, unless, as one southerner put it, "He has excluded himself. Some talk themselves out of it."

Republicans can also become, especially in committee and through the sufferance of the majority party, a part of the leadership of the entire Senate. Party lines are sufficiently dim to permit strong Republican influence on a few specific matters. Said a Democratic senator:

We all know there is constant consultation between the Majority and Minority Leaders. On the issues we pass on in the Senate we almost never have a strict party line vote and consequently there is consultation with and leadership exercised on the minority side in some degree. I don't think that the majority would ever start off by absolutely excluding the minority. I think they always talk with them and make some effort to have the leadership come from the minority side for whatever support the minority will lend. I think the minority leaders play an important part in legislation.

Democratic senators, then, look to various locations for leadership. They may look to the White House, the elected leadership, committee or subcommittee chairmen, or a network of generally respected senators, including a few Republicans. Virtually all senators, at least in the majority party, can aspire to lead on some matters. The formal leaders rapidly learn to live with a great deal of competition for the attention and loyalty of the members. Much of the "competitive" leadership activity, however, aims at results sought by the formal leaders.

The Republican View

The Republicans have a considerably different view of their leadership. They regard the formal leaders—and there are more of them in the Republican case—as much more important than Republican members of committees. This feeling is related to the high degree of activity and skill on the part of their Minority Leader, Everett Dirksen of Illinois. Dirksen generally overshadows Republicans with special expertise on committees. In 1964, for example, Dirksen named the seven Republican captains in charge of the different titles of the civil rights bill when it reached the floor, rather than letting them emerge naturally from the concerned committees.[4]

This feeling is also related to a general pattern of partisan inactivity and collusion with the Democratic chairmen on the part of most ranking Republican committee and subcommittee members. Senior Republicans on committees are less likely than senior Democrats to develop into "issue leaders." Hence the field is relatively clear for the formal leadership. At present, however, Republicans feel that there is less leadership activity than there should be for a minority party and that, although Dirksen is doing a fine job, he should not be called upon to operate almost alone.

The formal Republican leaders do not form a cohesive unit. Said one senior Republican, "The formal party leadership, like Topsy, just growed. We have a series of positions: the Chairman of the Republican Conference, the Chairman of the Republican Policy Committee, the Floor Leader, and the Assistant Floor Leader or

Whip. These men were not chosen at the same time, so there were particular reasons for the election of each."

The Republicans on committees develop into issue leaders only on relatively minor matters; the majority party monopolizes the important issues. Said one Republican,

I was supposed to be the man to see about a specific kind of legislation, at least for the people who were for the bill. Interestingly enough, when the number of Republicans shrank so much, these same people who used to come to me are now searching over on the Democratic side for a person to do that. I have also tried to make myself acquainted with another specific problem, so I assume some people will be talking to me when it comes up. But these are minor things. These aren't the great issues.

Republicans do not become "issue leaders" on important issues in part because of lack of numbers. Said one member, "We are spread thinner in the Senate than in the House. We don't get as much chance to specialize." Another reason for the lack of Republican leadership on specific issues is the nonpartisan style of many of the minority party's ranking members on committees. Said one Republican, in describing a specific situation:

A young fellow does have a frustrating experience. In connection with the Stockpile Subcommittee of Armed Services, I got very aroused by what seemed to me to be an effort of the Democrats to make hay out of the stockpile and the operation of it during the Eisenhower Administration. After I broke my neck on it and really pretty much accomplished just about what I thought was a fair thing, I ran into the ranking Republican on the committee. He was not inclined to fight about it; it was just not his nature. I talked with everybody; I secured outside legal advice; I spoke with some independent people; and was convinced by people with integrity that the Democrats were presenting a one-sided picture. This took weeks, but it came practically to nothing, because in the showdown I was standing practically by myself. Unless you are going to be fairly well supported in your own party you can't afford to do this kind of thing, since there are so many other things you have to do.

In the Republican party, then, there is less chance for an individual senator to become important to the whole Senate as an issue leader. He may, however, be an important issue leader within his own party. And there are, of course, exceptional cases in which a Republican will be a Senate-wide leader on an important matter. In 1967, for example, freshman senator Charles Percy of Illinois emerged as such an exception in the housing field. The necessities of minority status generally help create a situation in which there are a number of central leaders who share as best they can the duties and responsibilities of providing guidance on substance to all Republicans. When they choose not to provide such guidance, Republican senators may have to look to Democratic colleagues for issue leadership.

RESPONSIBILITY OF PARTY LEADERS

Democrats view their party leaders ideally as broadly responsible to the whole body of Democrats in the Senate, as well as to a Democratic President. There was, however, some disagreement over what responsibility meant in practice. Some felt that the leaders were in fact responsible to the Democratic Conference (all Democrats). Said one,

They [the members of the conference] select the leaders and the leaders are going to have a reasonably satisfied majority of them, or they are not going to be there next time, so in that sense I would say they are responsible. Mike Mansfield has stated on a number of occasions that he is accountable to the Democratic majority.

Others questioned whether this formal responsibility meant anything. They observed that the conference has never replaced a sitting Democratic leader and that reelection to leadership posts is automatic. Said one,

As a practical matter, the Democratic Conference meets very seldom. When it does, it is just for a rather broad presentation of some problem.

I don't think you could say that the leadership is held responsible to the Conference. It is just not conceivable to me that the Conference would meet and ask the Majority Leader to come before the Conference and answer for his conduct on something or other.

Republicans did not believe that their central leaders were held even formally responsible or accountable to the Republican Conference. They pointed out that Dirksen's predecessor as floor leader, William Knowland of California, was generally uncooperative and aloof, but that he was floor leader for five years and his tenure was terminated only by defeat at the polls, not by any action in the Republican Conference.

Republicans were concerned that they had no way of holding ranking Republicans on committees accountable for their actions and styles of operation. Said one Republican Senator:

The ranking member often, if not almost always, has been there in that spot for a long time. He has certain relations with the majority. They have a sort of a tacit understanding that on most things they are going to work out something that they can both support. This limits the younger people a great deal in their desire, which I have felt many times, to develop a good strong party alternative to whatever may be up there. The conclusion is plain enough: There is almost no effort at developing Republican positions.

The junior Republicans on committees have found no way to alter this situation. When House Republicans were frustrated by the same lack of accountability and activity on the part of ranking men and the minority party leaders, they ousted three party leaders and attempted to oust a fourth over a six-year period.[5] But such a course of action is unlikely among Senate Republicans. Each senator has several committees, and, if he is frustrated on one committee, he can devote his major attention to the work of another. Most senators are also extremely busy with nonlegislative chores; thus they do not worry as much as House members about their impact on party legislative positions.

STYLES OF LEADERSHIP IN THE CONTEMPORARY SENATE

Democrats

That there is no fixed style of operation that a floor leader must adopt is well illustrated by the contrast between Lyndon Johnson (floor leader, 1953-1961) and Mike Mansfield (floor leader, 1961-present).

Johnson operated "a highly personalized, intensive system of Senate rule adaptable to no successor." [6] He gradually developed control over a broad range of rewards and punishments, including committee assignments, office space, assignments to delegations scheduled to make foreign trips, campaign funds, the flow of information, and procedure. He relied heavily on unanimous consent agreements, aborted quorum calls, night sessions, and bursts of activity followed by periods of lethargy to move the Senate in directions he desired.

Crucial to Johnson's style was maintenance of a constant flow of information both to and from him. He wanted to know what all Democratic senators (and most of the Republicans) were thinking and doing. He reciprocated by telling them his plans for controlling the business of the Senate. Both in collecting and in distributing information Johnson relied heavily on Robert G. Baker, Secretary to the Majority.[7]

Democratic senators at the round tables described the Johnson-Baker information operation:

A: Bobby [Baker] kept you informed.
B: I'll say. He kept his finger on that legislation. He could tell you, "It will be safe for you to go home. I think it would be wise for you to go Thursday."
C: He knew the interests of the senators pretty well. He made it his business. So he would alert you ahead of time.
A: He would say, "You are interested in conservation. You better watch this bill."
D: Bobby worked at his job. There is no question. I would call Bobby. I would say, "Bobby, are we having a vote?" He would say, "I don't

know. I will call you." Or he would say, "I can't tell you; you just better stay," and nine times out of ten there would be a vote.

Baker also helped collect information for Johnson.

D: He would make floor polls and check you off. He had us on tab all the time. He would say, "Are you going to be interested in this bill? Are you going to be here?"
A: Or he would say, "Do you have any feelings about it?"
C: He passed the word along, so that once you talked with him and he knew, then you wouldn't be bothered anymore. Your position would be understood.

The Democratic participants said Johnson constantly checked their preferences and plans. He tried to sense dissent ahead of time and overcome it by negotiation. They viewed Johnson as an extremely aggressive — but conciliatory — Majority Leader. On the whole, his style of leadership met with favor because it got results. They liked the feeling of being led on some matters.

The Majority Leader since 1961, Mike Mansfield of Montana, is, in many ways, the opposite of Johnson. By nature he is unaggressive and unassuming. By choice, he often defers to the wishes of others in the party. At the round tables his fellow Democrats tended to view his leadership as lacking in many qualities they would have liked. The Democratic staff members who came to the round tables made a stronger case for the effectiveness of low-key leadership in the Senate.

Mansfield is uncomfortable with power. In discussing his Majority Leadership he said, "I have no power, no prestige, no influence." [8] He uses a "soft-sell." [9] Rather than meet a difficult issue head-on or even by deviousness he is likely to make straightforward compromises. For example, in 1964 he joined Dirksen in sponsoring a constitutional amendment that would have slowed the pace of legislative reapportionment. Mansfield did not like the proposal but commented that "It was a case of arriving at the best possible compromise in a question that is avalanching all over the country." It also allowed the Senate to consider adjourning, whereas a long fight would have made life in the Senate unpleasant by preventing a widely-desired adjournment.[10]

Two of his Democratic colleagues who attended the round tables disapproved of his style:

A: He is just very passive. He never takes any initiative. He doesn't make an effort to be a leader.

B: He doesn't try to put legislation over, as Johnson did.

A: He doesn't try to move it in a certain direction. He is a nice guy and everybody loves him, and all that sort of thing, but he isn't a leader.

One specific limit on Mansfield's effectiveness is the highly restricted use he makes of his position in relation to collecting and distributing information vital to the smooth working of the Senate. A leader who dominates the flow of information can strengthen his hand. A leader who ignores the flow of information weakens his position.

Democratic members of the round tables insisted that even though Mansfield and the Whip, Russell Long of Louisiana, went to the White House once a week they brought almost no infomation back with them that they were willing to distribute. Furthermore, Mansfield and Long do not collect much information about the activities and preferences of their fellow Democrats. Mansfield stopped the practice of taking detailed polls or head counts on specific bills. The White House does its own polling in the Senate. What Mansfield learns is from the White House, but there is no evidence to suggest that he even seeks this information.

Another limit on what Mansfield can accomplish is his lack of rapport with the Whip, Long. Between 1961 and 1965, Whip Hubert Humphrey of Minnesota engaged in some of the activities that Mansfield avoided. But Long seems little interested in the customary activities of a formal party leader. Rather he is intent on developing his powers as chairman of the Finance Committee to their fullest potential. His methods for increasing this power strike many Democratic senators as excessively crude and bullying.[11] He does not conceive the Whip's job to be one that automatically makes him a lieutenant of the President or the Administration or even the Majority Leader. In early 1967, for example, Long denied on national television that he spoke for the President or necessarily agreed with him. In his March 4, 1967, newsletter to his constituents he asserted his independence by cataloging his disagreements with the President (most of which were also disagreements with Mansfield) and by stating that the principal reason that he was glad to be Whip was that it put him in a position to do more for Louisiana.

The differences between Long and Mansfield are, however, rooted more in personal difficulties than in policy disagreements.[12] Their lack of regard for each other is apparent in the daily workings of the Senate. For example, their open clash over Long's plan for financing presidential campaigns involved a conflict between personalities, not just a dispute over policy.[13] Inside the Democratic party, their dispute has had two results growing out of Mansfield's determination not to give Long any real control over party affairs or over floor business. First, Mansfield appointed four Assistant Whips who could represent him on the floor, thus avoiding Long.[14] Second, the third ranking Democrat in the leadership, Conference Secretary Robert Byrd of West Virginia, has become Mansfield's principal assistant, again bypassing Long.

Despite his evident shortcomings as a leader, Mansfield can also be effective in specific situations. He uses three techniques particularly well.

First, he uses the unanimous-consent agreement even more frequently than Johnson did. This gives him great flexibility to motion up matters with no notice and have them passed with few senators on the floor. This at least allows him to keep the Senate from falling behind in its disposition of business unless some major matter produces a filibuster.[15]

Second, because Mansfield is particularly solicitous of the minority party's members and rights he can count on some support from them, if not on substance at least on procedure. And some of the major accomplishments of the Senate during Mansfield's tenure, such as the Civil Rights Act of 1964, have been achieved only through close bipartisan cooperation, especially between Mansfield and Dirksen. Republicans are much more generous in their assessment of Mansfield than Democrats. John Williams of Delaware, for example, said that "When Lyndon was the leader, he liked to play tricks on you. The game was always trying to outfox Lyndon. But I would never try to pull anything like that on Mike. Why, he'd just turn around and say, 'The Senator is perfectly within his rights . . .'" George Aiken of Vermont, the senior Republican in the Senate, said, "There isn't a Republican who would raise a finger to hurt Mike." [16]

Third, largely because of his interest in orderly scheduling, Mansfield has kept at least some subtle pressure on the standing committees to be productive. Democratic staff members at the round tables were convinced that this technique was particularly useful in 1965, when the votes were present for Democratic programs and thus scheduling and orderliness took on extra importance. Two committee staff members argued the case for Mansfield:

He writes a letter to the chairman asking what big bills will be out and then he follows it up with telephone calls. Mansfield has put contact with committees on a regular basis. First of all, he and the Policy Committee staff checked the President's program and then they asked the committee chairmen early about what the bills are and then they keep steadily checking on the progress of them.

The Democratic Policy Committee calls me once a week: 'When are you going to meet on this? When are you going to get this out? When are you going to do that?' So you can't say they are not exercising leadership. Nobody is more responsible for the President's program in the Senate than the Majority Leader. I think it is to Mr. Mansfield's credit that there isn't a lot of uproar on most of these bills.

The White House also made its own efforts to move legislation through the standing committees. Said one committee staff member, "Another thing that has been in evidence is White House calls.

There was a time when the White House called and every secretary receiving such a call passed out. Now, once a day you get a call from the White House about some matter that they want to check on independently."

Republicans

The Republicans at the round tables regarded themselves as individualists who would not submit to the blandishments of a leader. As a senior man put it, "I think this is the nature of the people who get elected as Republicans. We are loners. We are proud of our ability to make up our own minds. I don't know when the pattern began to develop, but it was here when I came and it has never been changed."

The Republican leaders take account of these preferences and operate much of the time without attempting to achieve unity. When the present leader, Dirksen, does seek unity, he avoids affronting any of the members by violating the basic individualistic norms.

The comments of the Republican senators on Knowland and Dirksen illustrate that, like the Democrats, the Republicans require no fixed style of their leaders.

Bill Knowland didn't talk to anybody. We never had any communication with Bill. He was running the Senate all by himself. This was partly Bill's makeup. He was a brusque individual.

I think Dirksen has done a superb job of really trying to hold his troops together. Seldom have I seen a fellow with as much tact and patience as he has with all kinds of fundamentally strong people and fundamentally difficult people. As a result, when he calls you and says, "I need some help on this; will you do it?" you say yes even though you may not completely agree with his viewpoint.

Dirksen has just persuaded me, as an individual, that he trusts me, and that I can trust him. If I go to him with a problem he will personally take care of it, if it is possible. I just feel very close to him, as an individual, and I will follow his leadership. I won't always vote with him, but usually do. He doesn't make many demands on us, but he is there for our service, and will give us the service, if he can.

Dirksen also appeared an effective leader to the Republican staff members at the round tables, although he operates on a highly personal basis and does not use machinery of the party, such as the Policy Committee and its staff. He does use a few of his own staff members for support.

In both parties, then, the present leaders respect the desires of individual senators to be left alone much of the time, free from party demands. This enhances the bargaining weight of the individual senators on those occasions on which the leaders do make demands. Senators of both parties view their leaders as helpful servants more than as masters.

PARTY COMMITTEES

Democratic Committees

STEERING COMMITTEE. The Democratic Steering Committee is chaired by the floor leader and composed of seventeen members. The floor leader also nominates all of his fellow members, who are automatically approved by the Democratic Conference. Sitting members automatically continue on the committee. Most of the members of the Steering Committee are quite senior. In 1966 eight of them were committee chairmen.

The Steering Committee, guided but not bound by seniority, votes on assignments of Democratic senators to committees. There is no formal geographical representation on the committee, and the access of individual Democrats to the committee varies radically. The Democratic participants in the round tables were interested in altering the Steering Committee to give each member specific geographic responsibilities, so that each Democratic senator would be represented by someone on the committee. The participants felt that the present general balance between conservatives and liberals and between northerners and southerners on the committee was good.

Mansfield, in the eyes of his colleagues, has less influence on the Steering Committee than did Lyndon Johnson. Bobby Baker helped

Johnson inspire applications for committees from the senators he favored for the openings.

POLICY COMMITTEE.[17] The Democratic Policy Committee is composed of nine senators and is chaired by the floor leader. He also appoints the members. Once a senator is made a member, he is automatically reappointed. The members of the committee are quite senior. Five of the nine members in 1966 were committee chairmen.

The job of the committee is to advise the Majority Leader on scheduling business for the floor, although it considers only some of the important bills. It has no power to veto bills that have been reported from standing committees; the final scheduling decision still lies with the Majority Leader. But it does give the Majority Leader some useful information on priorities, political considerations, and personal desires. Said one member of the Policy Committee:

We give the leadership a great deal of leeway. The Policy Committee might delay a bill. The members might ask the sponsor to come in and argue it, but I have never known the Policy Committee absolutely to block something, even when a majority may feel that the bill has little merit. From time to time, particularly at the precise request of some of the more senior conservative members, there were efforts to amend the bill before it goes to the floor. That is used quite rarely and selectively. They will dig into the merits from time to time, but it is not too often, really. A lot of the big stuff doesn't even go through the Policy Committee. The leader just takes it up as he wishes.

Occasionally, the Policy Committee will examine the substance of a bill. A non-committee member described his experience in defending a bill coming from his subcommittee: "I had to go in and defend over again all of the substantive parts of the bill the substantive committee had already decided on and reported, and I thought the Policy Committee was simply to schedule it for the time when it would come to the floor."

The senators were generally pleased with the present role and performance of the Policy Committee. They agreed that the committee's membership was not perfectly representative but that it was improving. Said one,

At one time it was quite heavily weighted, because of seniority and longevity, toward the South. In the last four years or so the additions have brought it pretty close to a balance. It is still heavily weighted with senior senators because here, like most everything else in the Senate, once you have achieved a position, you are never removed, and if a senator lives a long time, he will be on there.

This senator did not know his party history. Southerners were more heavily represented in 1965 than at any time in the preceding decade, as figures in Table XVIII reveal.

TABLE XVIII: SOUTHERN REPRESENTATION ON THE POLICY COMMITTEE, 1953-1965

YEAR	PERCENT OF SOUTHERNERS	
	Among all Senate Democrats	Among Policy Committee members
1953	47	33
1955	46	37
1957	45	33
1959	34	33
1961	34	23
1963	31	33
1965	29	44

The participants discussed the possibility of reorienting the work of the Policy Committee. When it was initially created, as a by-product of the Legislative Reorganization Act of 1946, it was supposed to do much more than just help the floor leader schedule business.[18] A senior member stated the original purpose:

The Policy Committee was supposed to fix the Democratic policy by which members could be judged as to loyalty and adherence to the party over a period of time, and to speak on the floor on these policies. The Reorganization Committee in 1946 came to the conclusion that parties are important, and party cohesion and party responsibility and party accountability are important, and it agreed that the only way to bring it about was by a Policy Committee that would be elected by each new

Congress and not be a carry-over and reflect the views of a Congress elected five or ten or twenty years ago, but reflect the views of the membership, and then fix party policy. Not that you would tell members how to vote, but you could judge them when they came up for a primary election by their adherence to a formally fixed party policy. You wouldn't try to get them to go along with the party, but it would be a scoreboard that you could go to the public with.

The round table members felt that a more active Policy Committee—even if not reconstituted every two years—could help in three different ways. First, its staff could provide Democratic members with more information on the substantive business of the Senate.

Second, the Policy Committee—if it formally stated party positions and kept records of members' agreement with and dissents from these positions—could provide some protective coloration in home states of individual senators. This would give the individual Democrats "something to tie to." Another senator agreed that it would provide help at home in explaining loyalty to the party, and added that he currently did the same thing by using *Congressional Quarterly* scores reflecting party support and opposition.

Third, a reactivated Policy Committee might strengthen the Senate position in negotiations over details in bills with the White House:

I wouldn't expect the Policy Committee to come out ever in direct opposition to the President, but since it would have senatorial ideas it might very well refine the situation between the administration and the Democratic majority in the Senate. It would be very helpful to the President sometimes. If he is running into bad weather on the Hill with his own party, a good Policy Committee could help to lead them into a compromise which would save the President's face, and also save the party's position. It is a linkage between the Executive and the Congress.

These comments reveal the individualistic orientation of the senators: each of the possible results represents primarily a service to them, not a strengthening of party.

CALENDAR COMMITTEE. For some years the Democrats had a three-man Calendar Committee that tried to keep the calendar moving in an orderly fashion and oversee it so that the interests of no individual senators were ignored or mistreated. In the last few years, however, the Calendar Committee has fallen into disuse. It is no longer composed of freshmen members with the time to spend on the floor. Furthermore, Mansfield's style of handling floor business —which involves picking and choosing, apparently at random, among bills ready for floor action—does not lend itself to review by a Calendar Committee. However, there was some feeling among the Democratic participants that this committee had earlier served the useful purpose of informing individual senators about the schedule and should be resuscitated.

CONFERENCE. The Democratic Conference is the formal name for all Democratic senators meeting together. It has a chairman (the Majority Leader) and a secretary. In the past, when it sometimes met as a caucus and made binding decisions, this group has had an important policy impact. During the first two years of Woodrow Wilson's presidency (1913-1915) the caucus reached its high point of activity. At that time it met, discussed issues and amendments on the major points of Wilson's legislative program, and took binding positions that guaranteed the success of those programs on the floor.[19] But since that time it has steadily declined in influence. At present, and for the past two or three decades, it has generally met only at the beginning of each Congress to ratify the present leadership's tenure in office or to elect new leaders if vacancies have occurred. The last successful attempt to oust an incumbent leader in this conference came in 1913.

Occasionally the conference will meet to discuss substantive matters, but not to take a party position. The Democrats at the round table testified that few senators came to these informal meetings, and when they did it was generally because there was disagreement over the best course of action on a specific matter.

One exception to this pattern was described:

You will recall, we had a conference or two on the possibility of a railroad strike. I think that brought about a firming up of opinion—no definite legislation, but we had to do something, and we were on the spot, so we

got behind the chairman. The chairman of the committee having jurisdiction asked the leadership to call the meeting to get a consensus of
Democrats. There was a necessity for action. We might not like what
we were going to do, but we had to do something. There was no effort
to bind the members, but just to outline the seriousness of it and to
get the strategy.

Republican Committees

COMMITTEE ON COMMITTEES. The Republican leaders designate the chairman and members of the Committee on Committees.
The full Conference of Republicans then automatically ratifies these
choices. Except for the chairman, the members ordinarily serve only
two years. The chairman, according to one senator, is usually "a
rather senior senator. It has been someone who has been universally
admired for fairness. Everybody respects him."

The committee's main function is to record preferences of senators
and then allocate openings strictly on the basis of seniority. Its suggestions are formally approved by the full Republican Conference.
It has some modest weight in preventing possible conflicts over assignments.

POLICY COMMITTEE.[20] The Republican Policy Committee in
the Senate has developed along different lines from the Democratic
Policy Committee. It has developed a staff, numbering eighteen in
1965, to help Republican senators with research on substantive matters.

The Policy Committee in 1965 was composed of eight party leaders and six Republican senators facing campaigns in 1966. The party
leaders are automatically on the committee. The other members are
nominated by the chairman of the Republican Conference and rati-
fied by the conference.

The Policy Committee staff is, as one senator put it, "the party's
staff in the Senate for general services, general research, reports on
legislation, and development of material that could be used in campaigns."

The senators on the committee do not take party positions. They apparently do not meet as a committee. But the one project they undertake is to hold a lunch every Tuesday to which all Republican senators are invited.

A staff man described these meetings:

It is completely informal. Senators Dirksen (Minority Leader), Hickenlooper (Chairman of the Policy Committee), and Saltonstall (Chairman of the Conference), in a sense, preside. Senator Dirksen gives a picture of what is coming up, some of the main issues as well. Senator Hickenlooper takes over for a certain area, Senator Saltonstall for another and then they ask for reports from other senators from their committees and pending legislation and what the problem may be and then it is a free-for-all discussion on many things.

CONFERENCE. The Republican Conference includes all Republican senators, who elect their own chairman. In past years the conference has never been as important as was the Democratic Conference in 1913-1915. But it has usually held some meetings each year on policy matters and occasionally will attempt to state a party position, although such a position is not regarded as formally binding on individual Republican senators. In 1964, for example, the conference passed a resolution supporting the civil rights bill. In the final roll call on the floor, thirty Republicans voted for it and none against.

The Republican Conference, formally constituted, meets about six to eight times a year. At the formal meetings, organizational matters are often the topic of conversation. In 1965, for instance, the conference met two or three times on the proposed change in the seniority rule for committee assignments. It also meets on important legislative matters about three or four times a year. According to the round table participants, about 60 or 70 percent of the Republican senators attend these meetings. Two Republican senators discussed the nature of the meetings:

A: Senator Saltonstall (the conference chairman) always makes it very clear that nobody is going to be asked to commit himself.

B: Would it be fair to say a conference comes together when it looks as though there might be sufficient deviation of opinions among the Republicans, and it is a good idea to get ironed out at a conference?

A: I think so. Senator Saltonstall has been very cooperative. I think when any Republican senator feels that he has a subject of sufficient importance to ask for a conference, Senator Saltonstall tries to accommodate him, or talk him out of it. At the meeting itself there are usually one or two individuals who may have a keen interest and many have asked for the conference, and they usually take the lead in expressing themselves, but after you get past that, it is open for general discussion.

IMPACT OF THE PARTY LEADERS

A summary of the impact of party leadership in the late 1940's and early and mid-1950's is still generally accurate for the Senate of the mid-1960's:

On Capitol Hill everyone is a partisan. Yet the Democratic and Republican parties are quite different in the Senate. The Democrats incline toward a highly personalized rule by the floor leader; the Republicans, toward leadership by a handful of party officials. In neither party do the leaders conceive of their jobs as regularly requiring the development of an over-all legislative program or regular intervention into committee proceedings. Rather, their principal efforts are directed toward maximizing party unity during the floor consideration and voting on bills. . . .

Party unity in the Senate is more the result of the correspondence of views of the senator and the actions of his party than the result of "pressure" from the leadership. However, the party leaders do have an effect on their parties' unity.[21]

Senators of both parties expect the party leaders to perform three main tasks. First, the leaders should state party positions on at least some legislative matters. The party leaders are viewed by many members as legitimate agents for taking party positions. Others insist that the party leaders should state a position only if a consensus in the party is present. Democrats saw their party leaders as spokesmen rather than molders of party positions. On the most important matters the leaders echoed the position taken by the

President. On less important matters, party policy was decided in the standing committees by the Democratic members. The job of the leader was to enforce the work of the standing committees and present their legislative product as something that the party should endorse. Republicans, on the other hand, felt that Dirksen had a little more room for independent action but that he, too, was largely a spokesman, principally for the senior Republicans on standing committees.

Second, the members expect their leaders to make appeals for unity and loyalty on important bills. They do not, however, accept coercion as legitimate, nor do they think that the party leaders should interfere with the business of standing committees, aside from urging them to keep on schedule.

The typical appeal from Democratic leaders was, in the words of one member, "Can you help me out; we would like to get this passed." Johnson and Mansfield differed in personal style, but they both used noncoercive persuasion and appeal. Two members summarized the Johnson style:

A: He was in the cloak room or other places all the time.
B: He circulated.
A: He had his arm around you. He would say, "Beloved, can you help me?" You got the feeling that you would like to help him.

Another senator described the Mansfield style:

Mansfield is very gentle, but he will sometimes call a meeting of some eight or ten senators and have coffee and cookies in his office, and just talk over the legislation that is coming up and without making an outright plea, this can still probably be diagnosed as some sort of a pep meeting. This is the very soft sell for the Administration's position. He wants to get everybody together: "Let's don't have too many amendments, and we can't waste too much time on getting this bill passed."

Dirksen also uses a noncoercive appeal. He asks people to trust his judgment on a personal basis and to support his policy stands when possible. The potential weapons in the hands of the leadership

—control over some limited campaign funds and control over committee assignments—are not, according to the Republicans, used to enforce party discipline on legislative matters.

Third, members of both parties expect their leaders both to distribute and to collect information on scheduling and on substance. Senators feel that the leaders operate somewhat haphazardly in this respect, but they do not demand a more carefully organized system. Democrats indicated, however, that they would like more advance notice on scheduling. Republicans, in contrast, felt that their Tuesday luncheons under Policy Committee sponsorship sufficed to distribute information to all senators. As one Republican put it, "At least there is a weekly contact with the leadership, face to face, and an opportunity to discuss the immediately pending legislation." Aside from the information dispensed at this weekly meeting, most information from the central leadership was likely to come from the Senate Minority Secretary. No members of either party felt that the leaders systematically collected information about what was going on in the Senate; however, they generally found the existing situation satisfactory.

The leaders of both parties in the present Senate play a limited role in restricting the options and choices of individual members. They clearly receive less deference and have a smaller impact on the members than the leaders in the House.[22] Individual senators are content with this situation. They are willing to make changes in the leadership structure and operations if the changes will enhance their own position, but the members have almost no concern for the strength of their parties as such. Greater power in the hands of the leaders might mean diminished power in the hands of individual senators.

Notes

[1] For information on the nature of the round table discussions see Appendix A. In addition to the 17 senators and 30 staff members who participated in the round tables I also conducted personal interviews with 11 senators and 19 staff

members on a variety of specific subjects. In addition, I had access to six lengthy open-ended interviews with senators conducted for a Westinghouse Broadcasting Corporation series on Congress. Most of these additional interviewees did not attend the round tables.

[2] See Roger H. Davidson, David M. Kovenock, and Michael K. O'Leary, *Congress in Crisis: Politics and Congressional Reform* (Wadsworth, 1966), pp. 153-154.

[3] See Martin Nolan, "Muskie of Maine," *Reporter*, July 13, 1967, pp. 44-46.

[4] *Washington Post*, March 8, 1964.

[5] In 1959 Charles Halleck ousted Joseph Martin as Minority Leader. In 1963 Gerald Ford defeated Charles Hoeven as Conference Chairman. In 1965 Ford replaced Halleck as Minority Leader. Also in 1965 Peter Frelinghuysen was unsuccessful in challenging Leslie Arends for the post of Whip.

[6] Rowland Evans and Robert Novak, *Lyndon B. Johnson: The Exercise of Power* (New American Library, 1966), p. 95. See chapter 6 for an excellent general discussion of the "Johnson System." Comments here are based in part on that discussion. See also Ralph K. Huitt, "Democratic Party Leadership in the Senate," *American Political Science Review*, Vol. 55 (June 1961), pp. 333-344.

[7] Baker continued some of his informational activities under Mansfield, but resigned the job in 1963 after various financial irregularities had been charged against him.

[8] *Sunday Star* (Washington), January 8, 1967.

[9] For a fine discussion of Mansfield's style see the story by Andrew J. Glass in the *Washington Post*, September 25, 1966.

[10] See the *Washington Post*, August 13, 1964.

[11] See the *Wall Street Journal*, May 2, 1967; and the *Sunday Star* (Washington), May 7, 1967.

[12] For one version of a key incident leading to the break between Mansfield and Long see the *Washington Post*, September 25, 1966. "Mansfield was appalled when, during the final night of last year's Senate session . . . Long, having dined well but not wisely, had to be carried out of the chamber, flush-faced, by three of his brawny colleagues. . . . Well-informed senators contend the incident triggered a break with Long that cannot be repaired."

[13] See the *Washington Post*, April 21, 1967; and the *Evening Star* (Washington), April 22, 1967.

[14] See the Evans and Novak column in the *Washington Post*, January 19, 1966.

[15] Mansfield has used this technique throughout his period as Majority Leader. See, for example, Floyd M. Riddick, "The Eighty-seventh Congress: First Session," *Western Political Quarterly*, Vol. 15 (June 1962), p. 261.

[16] Quotations are from the *Washington Post*, September 25, 1966.

[17] See Hugh A. Bone, *Party Committees and National Politics*. (University of Washington Press, 1958), chapter 6; Bone, "An Introduction to the Senate Policy Committees," *American Political Science Review*, Vol. 50 (June 1956), pp. 229-359; and Malcolm E. Jewell, *Senatorial Politics and Foreign Policy* (University of Kentucky Press, 1962).

[18] On the compromises surrounding the Legislative Reorganization Act of

1946 that allowed the Senate to set up policy committees see Joseph Cooper, *Reorganization and Reform in the House of Representatives* (forthcoming).

[19] On this period see Randall B. Ripley, *Majority Party Leadership in Congress* (Little, Brown, 1969), chapter 3.

[20] See Bone, *Party Committees:* Bone, "An Introduction to the Senate Policy Committees"; Jewell, *op. cit.;* and Jewell, "The Senate Republican Policy Committee and Foreign Policy," *Western Political Quarterly,* Vol. 12, (December 1959), pp. 966-980.

[21] Donald R. Matthews, *U.S. Senators and Their World* (University of North Carolina Press, 1960), p. 145.

[22] See Randall B. Ripley, *Party Leaders in the House of Representatives* (Brookings, 1967).

Chapter 5: **The Committee System: Chairmen, Ranking Minority Members, and Conference Committees**

The senior Democrat and the senior Republican on each of the sixteen standing committees in the Senate do not have as much institutional power as their counterparts in the House, but they are highly important and visible individuals. Except in a few cases, they use the power that comes to them through institutional position and the power they develop through their personal skills in order to become more powerful than the other individual senators on their committee.[1] Typically, especially in the case of the chairman, they tend to head the coalition that prevails on the most important decisions that the full committee makes. At present, these men tend to be more powerful on most issues than the formal party leaders.

But, given the dispersion of power to individuals in their subcommittee roles and given the autonomy of most subcommittees, they are not powerful enough to warrant calling the Senate decentralized instead of individualistic.

THE POWER AND POSITION OF CHAIRMEN

Sources of Power for Chairmen

Most chairmen face little opposition to their wishes inside their committees. This condition may exist because they have independent power with which they can dominate the committee members. It may also be because they are faithfully reflecting the preferences of either the majority of the committee or a few powerful members of the committee. Chairmen are not automatically imbued with power or compelled to be active. The title "chairman," like the title "majority leader," does not prescribe a set pattern of behavior.

The Banking and Currency Committee offers a good example of chairmen with radically different styles successively chairing the same committee.[2] In the Republican Eighty-third Congress (1953-1954), Homer Capehart, Indiana Republican, chaired the committee. Capehart devoted most of his time to committee work, supervised all of the major committee activities, and did not allow power to be exercised independently by subcommittees.

Capehart's successor, J. William Fulbright, Arkansas Democrat, chaired the committee from 1955 until the middle of the Eighty-sixth Congress (1959), when he became chairman of the Foreign Relations Committee, a job in which he was much more interested personally. During his tenure as chairman of Banking and Currency, Fulbright developed a strong staff and parceled out power over different subjects to subcommittees. The committee became essentially a collection of subcommittees and the chairman's main concern was with scheduling and efficiency, not with substance. He became, at least for his fellow Democrats, a "service chairman."

A. Willis Robertson, a conservative Democrat from Virginia, became chairman in 1959 and remained through the Eighty-ninth

Congress (1965-1966). His main interest was in banking legislation, and he retained substantial control over the committee's activities in this area. He opposed the majority views on the committee in some other fields—such as housing, aid to mass transit, and aid to depressed areas—but did not try to block absolutely the preferences of the majority of the members. Instead he played a "minority and restraining" role, hindering actions he did not like where he could but acquiescing where he could not hinder without an all-out and bitter struggle.

A chairman's style and power are partially determined by the inner discipline and cohesion of his committee. Senator Fulbright, as chairman of Foreign Relations, is hampered by the disparate points of view on policy questions publicly stated by the members of his committee. He is also hampered by his disagreements with the White House. Thus he is rarely consulted by the White House on matters of concern to him and is not even routinely consulted by the Senate leaders. In 1965, for example, Senator Mansfield did not consult Fulbright before he announced that he was postponing consideration of the consular treaty with the Soviet Union. By contrast, Senator John Stennis, Mississippi Democrat, wields substantial power as chairman of the Preparedness Subcommittee of the Armed Services Committee because the members of that subcommittee typically speak, at least publicly, with a single voice.[3]

Chairmen are accorded deference in part because the junior members of the committee hope to be reelected often enough to achieve seniority and chairmanships themselves. The juniors, therefore, are often reluctant to participate in any activity that might permanently decrease the power, prestige, or position of the chairmanship. They want to inherit undiminished powers and perquisites.

A chairman also gains power because he usually knows more about the subject before his committee than anyone else, and other members are often compelled to go to him for accurate information. Usually he can present this information as a persuasive case for doing whatever it is he wants.

Also inhibiting opposition to the chairman is the debt most members owe him for past favors or their anticipation of a day when they will need something from him. Chairmen possess eight types of essentially procedural power that allow them to grant or withhold "favors" or "somethings."

First, the chairman controls the agenda of the committee and the scheduling of business, including hearings. The individual member is, therefore, largely dependent on the chairman if he wants any particular piece of legislation moved through the committee. Said one Republican senator:

> If a member were to bring up a bill which the chairman didn't want on the agenda that week, the chairman would usually be supported by a majority. Some chairmen simply say, "I am not going to bring it up," and that involves an appeal from the decision of the chair, which is rarely taken and would be more rarely successful. Also, the chairman has the sole right in the committees on which I serve, in the setting of hearings on any given legislation. So he has the power to call up bills, the power to designate the hearing dates, the power to call an executive session for the purpose of reporting the bill out. There are technical defenses against this power, but, in my experience, they don't work.

A Democratic staff member elaborated on the same point:

> The real source of the chairman's power as a practical matter, in our committee is that he schedules the meetings and he schedules the committee's program. He schedules the executive sessions and makes up the agenda. Or he approves the agenda the staff puts together for him. So by doing this you have tremendous power in saying when you are and are not going to meet, or if you are going to go out on field hearings or are not going to go out on field hearings.

In 1959 for example, James Eastland, Mississippi Democrat and chairman of the Judiciary Committee, was able to prevent action in his committee on a civil rights bill. Parliamentary maneuvering by Eastland and his fellow southerners on the committee wasted much time. Typically, the committee met only 90 minutes each Monday, and this time would be given to a rambling speech by a single southerner.[4] In 1960 the leaders had to bypass the committee altogether through the device of a nongermane amendment to a minor bill on the floor in order to obtain action on a civil-rights bill.

Second, the chairman typically has effective control over all or most of the staff for both the full committee and subcommittees. Men who have been granted a staff member by the chairman or plan to seek one from him are not likely to lead revolts against the chairman's plans for committee action or inaction. Robertson, for example, kept the Banking and Currency Committee staff small to promote inaction.

Third, the chairman assigns the members of his party to subcommittees and juggles the number and composition of subcommittees. A subcommittee chairman or a man who hopes to be a subcommittee chairman needs to remain in the good graces of the chairman. The testimony of one Democrat highlights what can happen to a dissenter.

I was removed from a subcommittee as chairman because I wasn't in accord with the views of the chairman of the full committee. He just announced what the subcommittee lines were going to be. I protested and asked for a hearing. He said the reason I was removed was that he wanted to have a senior member move back in there. But that wasn't his real reason.

Senator Robertson protected the dominance of his view of the Federal Reserve System within the Banking and Currency Committee by simply abolishing the Federal Reserve Subcommittee when the chairman who agreed with him was defeated in the 1960 election. Two liberal Democrats much more critical of the System were in line for and desired the chairmanship. Robertson transferred the responsibilities of the subcommittee to the full committee, in which he would preside.[5]

Some chairmen, however, voluntarily bind themselves by seniority in establishing subcommittees, thereby abnegating part of their power.

Fourth, chairmen—even those who pick subcommittee chairmen

strictly by seniority—have a large measure of control over the budgets allocated to their subcommittees. This control can keep a subcommittee chairman from making the impact he desires if he is not in accord with the chairman. Robertson, for example, allocated funds sparingly in order to limit the activities and impact of subcommittees.

Fifth, a committee chairman has the power, in most cases, to designate which senators, at least of his own party, are to go on foreign trips. A Republican senator described how a cooperative chairman adds to his power by the use of control over foreign travels.

He is most cordial and cooperative if some member wants to attend a delegation meeting in Geneva, Oslo, or some other place. I think that ought to be mentioned because it is one of the sources of the chairman's power. This is important to those senators who like to travel. The chairman has a right to say whether or not he thinks members of the committee should or should not travel, and generally controls the course of their conduct abroad.

Sixth, the chairman can be extremely useful to the members of his committee by protecting them from controversial issues that may involve some electoral danger. One Republican senator spoke candidly:

All members of Congress have the not-so-worthy instinct for self-preservation, expressed in the desire to avoid as long as they can the toughest questions. The committee system and the committee chairman's power can be used to protect you from having to face these questions. These can be relatively small things like anti-vivisection laws or temperance questions—which were important at one time. And a lot of people don't want to face things of this sort, and so they acquiesce in a system which makes it possible for hard choices to be avoided in many cases.

Seventh, chairmen can offer the role of principal sponsor of important legislation to an individual member of a committee or subcommittee. This increases the member's visibility and prestige both inside and outside of the Senate.

Eighth, chairmen appoint conferees, thereby giving an individual member a last chance to fight for his particular interests on a bill. If he is not a member of the conference committee he may well find that the provisions for which he had worked are deleted or severely amended as the price of agreement with the House conferees.

The Chairmen and Committee Procedure

The formal rules of Senate committees are of little interest to most senators. They are aware that the powers of the chairmen are enhanced by the lack of rules. But they are content with the distribution of power within most committees, because virtually all of them have attained some standing on at least one subcommittee that interests them. Thus, except in unusual cases, they are not troubled because others, principally the chairman, may have more power. They have enough to pacify them at the present and, given reelection and good health, they anticipate that increasing seniority will bring increasing power.

Because most senators at present obtain at least part of their legislative preferences without being hampered by their chairman, they maintain that at least a rough approximation of majority rule prevails in all committees. Said one western Democrat, "My experience has been that whether there are specific committee rules or not, a majority has a chance to work its will in Senate committees. I think that in the Senate a determined majority can pass legislation and can get legislation reported."

Only one Democrat at the round tables indicated that the lack of rules and set procedures might make the internal committee operations less than fully democratic.

The committee chairman seems to have complete power himself to decide whether a bill will go to one subcommittee or another, or whether he will keep it in the whole committee. That, in effect, says whether he wants to control it completely. If he keeps it in the whole committee, it means he is going to keep it tightly within his grasp. If he gives it to a given subcommittee, it is because he wants it handled that way by that subcommittee chairman or another subcommittee.

Other Democratic senators immediately indicated that they knew of no committee that operated like this. They observed that most committees had a set procedure for referring bills to subcommittees that did not allow the chairman any arbitrary power.

The Republicans showed no particular interest in the rules either. One senator felt that written rules might guarantee the rights of the minority more securely against the stacking of hearings by an unfair chairman. But this situation did not occur often enough to be intolerable.

Staff members from both parties shared many of the senators' perceptions, although they put greater stress on the *limited* nature of the democracy in most committees. The Democratic staff members thought that chairmen were limited by the necessities of consent and accommodation, not by formal rules. But they also indicated that a chairman can set the procedural style for a committee and has a free hand on many matters that do not reach the limits of consent and accommodation.

If you can get the chairman to agree to a meeting you can have a democratic one.

There are a number of situations where a chairman can get something that he wants very badly even if the committee feels basically the other way.

My chairman has learned the technique of voting the proxies when it is going against him.

The other day in an instance in our committee it was almost the way Abraham Lincoln had his cabinet meeting. The chairman polled the members and everybody was against him and his was the only aye vote and he said, "The ayes have it." The other members listened and they didn't have too much to say to the chairman because he was convinced that the bill we were about to act on shouldn't be acted on at that time, and it wasn't acted on.

Despite these powers of the chairman, the Democratic staff members agreed that no chairman could stop the progress of an important bill for very long if the majority of the committee favored it. But on less important bills and when faced by unmobilized majorities, chairmen wield great, even absolute, power.

The staff members viewed their own job as one of facilitating the atmosphere of consent and accommodation on legislative matters before committees. The staff must keep the channels of communication clear between people who might disagree if they did not consent beforehand.

Chairmen can also foster an atmosphere of consent. One Democratic Committee staff member said,

Our chairman will defer to any member who really wants to delay action on something, but the first time that member starts to give somebody else a hard time on delaying something, then he is in trouble. Everybody is expected to play by the same rules and the result of this is that the chairman is in the position of umpiring the game.

As a result, the limits prescribed by the consensual and accommodating pattern of committee action are rarely reached. There are few explosions to disturb the serene proceedings in most committees.

The chairman, of course, does not have strong views on all of the important matters before his committee. He can use his position to facilitate the maximum amount of agreement before the committee makes its final decision by formally voting. Said one Democratic staff member:

For the most part the chairman of the committee is not locked into a specific role that is apart from the rest of the committee. So when he comes into a meeting it isn't a question of listening to somebody and then deciding whether to give him what he wants. There is usually a group that pretty generally are in accord on what they are trying to get out of the committee and there may be one or a group of people who are opposed and want to modify it. Generally, it is a give and take, back and forth, which in our case the chairman lets go until it begins to bog down. Then he will ask if everybody is ready to vote and try to push it to a vote or try to push it over.

A staff member from a different committee added:

There are very few surprises in a committee. You know in advance and you try to reach an accommodation well before. There are very, very few times when you really reach a head-on collision inside a committee. Generally when you do, both sides understand exactly what is at stake and how far they can go in it.

Because senators sit on several committees the chances and necessity for negotiation are increased. The senators' remembering that they will have to deal with other specific senators on a number of issues facilitates accommodation.

Republican staff members also stressed the importance of accommodation in committee work. Said one man,

The club-like atmosphere is more true of subcommittees than of the Senate floor as a whole. Somebody who is not necessarily a member of the Senate establishment, whatever that is, on the Senate floor, might very well be a leading figure in the club of a particular subcommittee in which he has tremendous interest and background and ability. Related to this is the lack of committee rules.

This club-like atmosphere in a committee can disintegrate rapidly when a question dividing the parties arises. Then the majority Democrats do not hesitate to engage in a number of procedural maneuvers to win their point and go on to something else. One Republican staff member identified "the barrel of proxies" as a technique used by the majority party. Others indicated that the Democrats are adroit at getting a quorum for a moment, then letting it disappear but still being able to win because of proxies. Only a few committees limit the use of proxies.

One of the few Senate committees with written rules is Banking and Currency. These rules were adopted because liberals of both parties resented the way the chairman was handling the committee. However, the rules have not substantially altered the operations of the committee. The basic limits on the chairman are still those of accommodation. The existence of written rules is a reminder that a former chairman overstepped those limits.

Checks on the Power of Chairmen

The many sources of power for chairmen do not give them absolute power. Not all chairmen possess personalities equally suited to the use of power. A Republican senator discussed a chairman whose personal traits rendered him ineffective:

He finds it very difficult to control his committee and get them to do anything he wants. His power is outside the Congress. He has a committee of diverse views and temperament. I won't say the committee is demoralized, but it does not function. He will not change his mind or subordinate his own views. He has ideas on what should be done, but he does not know how to handle his committee members to get the maximum cooperation from them. And they vote him down. He is quite stubborn. He was not born to be a chairman. He is a philosopher.

Some chairmen also voluntarily limit their power because they have agreeable personal relations with members whose views differ from their own. Or the disagreeing members may, through personal charm and skill, disarm a hostile chairman. Edward Kennedy, a liberal Massachusetts Democrat, seems able to get much of what he wants on the Judiciary Committee from Chairman Eastland, despite completely antithetical positions on most questions coming before the committee, largely because of the effective personal relations he has established with Eastland. He does not react to Eastland's occasional public denunciations of him because he realizes that Eastland is speaking to the (white) folks back home. When he defeats Eastland on civil rights or immigration or criminal penalties for violations of State Department travel restrictions, he does it graciously and without insulting the loser. Thus he is accorded courtesies by Eastland inside the committee that a gloating victor would not get. For example, Eastland gave Kennedy the right to sit on a subcommittee of which he was not a member even though Eastland knew that Kennedy wanted to come to oppose a pet project of his own. He even relinquished the chair of his own sub-committee to Kennedy to preside over consideration of a bill that Eastland bitterly opposed.[6]

Party leaders occasionally limit the power of chairmen. Much more frequently in the contemporary Senate the individual senators on a committee find ways of limiting power that is obnoxious to them. Many of these limits are only potential rather than actual, but they are used often enough to persuade chairmen of the wisdom of restraint.

Committee members may, for example, outvote a chairman in committee. There is always a potential threat against a chairman with only marginal control over his committee. Said one Democratic senator, "I think in almost all committees over a period of two years, the chairman will lose some ground. Legislation will get out he doesn't approve of or legislation will be changed, contrary to his views. If he is a smart chairman, he will smile, relax and enjoy it."

Outvoting a chairman often takes parliamentary skill and perseverance. In 1958, for example, Paul Douglas, Illinois Democrat, was faced with a situation in which it looked as if the chairman of the Banking and Currency Committee, Fulbright, had made it impossible for legislation on aid to depressed areas to be reported favorably. Douglas chaired a subcommittee that was stacked against the bill, although there was at least the potential of a bipartisan coalition in favor of the bill in the full committee. Once Douglas had solidified such a coalition, he then forced Fulbright, in a procedural showdown involving a formal vote of the committee, to bring the bill to the full committee rather than allowing it to languish in the subcommittee.[7]

Chairmen may also be forced to make compromises on substance or scheduling without reaching the showdown of a formal vote. In 1965, for example, Chairman Robertson yielded on an important amendment in committee in order to attain rapid consideration of his bank-merger bill. Without the concession, the liberals on his committee could have slowed its passage and possibly prevented its success altogether.[8]

Another potential curb on the powers of committee chairmen lies in the internal rules adopted and used by Senate committees. Most committees have deliberately not adopted rules, and what rules they have are generally ignored. Said one Democratic staff member, "Every rule made indicates a breakdown of civility and the Senate is a very civil institution." Another Democratic staff member indicated that the chairman can create an illusion of operating under definite rules. "We have no rules in our committee except when the chairman needs them. The expert on the rules is the Chief Clerk and he makes them on the spur of the moment. The chairman will say, 'What's the committee rule on that?' and he will have to have an answer. God help him if they ever want to see it in writing."

Despite the flexibility or nonexistence of committee rules, most chairmen will not go so far as to provoke a procedural showdown with the members of their committee. A skillful chairman can avoid most controversy that will lead to a diminution of his power by compromising enough to keep potential opposition disarmed. Said one Democratic staff member:

If matters come to a head, there has been a serious breakdown somewhere. We have seventeen members of the committee and if twelve or thirteen come to the chairman and say, "Mr. Chairman, we want to meet on this bill," the chairman knows what the score is, and then something will be done. He will amend it the way he wants it amended or something of that nature. He will carefully avoid surprises.

Another check on the power of committee chairmen is the ability of the Senate as a whole to bypass a committee and bring a bill directly to the floor without committee action. This was done, for example, in order to pass civil rights legislation in 1960 and 1964. Or the Senate can give a bill to a committee, with instructions that it be reported out on a certain day or within a certain time period. This was done in the case of the 1965 voting rights bill.

Dissenting members of a committee can also make an appeal on the floor of the Senate if they disagree with the chairman and the majority of the committee on substantive positions contained in a bill that has been reported. This sanction, of course, is not present if the committee has refused to report a specific bill. This kind of appeal has limited chances of success because few senators listen to floor debates and most automatically vote the position taken by their fellow party members on the standing committee handling the bill.

Even when a chairman loses a round in the Senate, he is customarily defeated in a way that leaves his reputation and power undamaged for the future. This is in sharp contrast to the House, where in the last fifteen years several well-publicized battles have been fought for committee control. When a House chairman lost in one of these disputes, his power was gone. In the Senate, according to a Democratic staff member, "Where there has been head-on conflict between the chairman and the rest of the committee, there was a well-planned-out ritual in most cases. The chairman doesn't really lose power as a result of the conflict."

Assessment: The Use of Power by Chairmen

The general feeling of the round table participants was that most chairmen were reasonable in their use of power, largely because they are kept in check by the general norms of compromise, mutual adjustment, and civility that give form and cohesiveness to Senate life. Members of both parties agreed that there has been a decrease in stubborn, dictatorial committee chairmen in the last several decades.

A chairman can have the mannerisms of a despot, but he no longer has despotic power. If his committee is strongly opposed to his position, he will probably lose. But despotic flourishes by the chairman can sometimes intimidate potential opponents so that they will not coalesce or will not make the determined effort necessary to defeat him. Two Democrats illustrated this in a discussion about the chairman of a committee on which they both serve.

A: This committee is a very frustrating committee to be on.
B: There is no deliberation.
A: No, the Chairman comes in; he is a real despot; he has already set his opinion; he makes snide remarks about people with different viewpoints. He turns to the ranking Republican, snorts at the Democrats, and he is, to my idea, just a terrible chairman. He bangs the gavel down, closes debate and so on. But his attitude toward any lowly one is, "You are dirt."
He gets apoplexy and pouts and says, "I am going to leave and let the next man take over. He is going to be the chairman anyhow. I am quitting," and he acts like a spoiled child.
B: There is a running feud between the chairman and a senior Democrat but the chairman usually wins. In the long run, however, the chairman generally lets the committee decide.
A: If you can put up with it.
B: He can make it awfully nasty, so you might retreat from the confrontation.

On the basis of their seniority and their expertise on specific subjects most chairmen become at least a transient part of the party leadership. Because of the natural tendency of senators on the floor to follow the committee position (which is, despite the exceptions cited, usually the chairman's position) they have natural and almost inevitable weight in at least some subject matter areas; and they may develop weight in other areas. Said one Democrat, "Chairmen are a sort of rump part of the leadership. They go in and out, depending on their interests." Another Democrat went farther: "I can't think of any person not a committee chairman about whom I would say, 'He is an influential part of the leadership.'" But most took a more moderate view that chairmen are automatically important in their own subject areas but not necessarily leaders in any other sense.

The Democratic senators generally preferred the accommodating type of chairman. No chairman in power at the time of the round tables (1965) seemed completely unreasonable to them. As members of the majority party they found satisfaction in a committee assignment even if the chairman attempted to be arbitrary. As chairmen or as important members of subcommittees, they could wield substantial power even under a difficult chairman. They criticized some specific chairmen. But most of the Democrats—even the more junior liberals—were willing to work within the system and did not wish to change it.

The Republicans talked about the requirements for a good chairman from the minority party point of view. The minority members have fewer channels for self-expression on a committee, and an unfair chairman can clog those channels. A good chairman, therefore, gives fair and equal treatment to all members, especially by reasonable use of rules and procedures. He schedules hearings on bills proposed by the minority. He knows his subject.

The Republicans also had a more philosophical reason for favoring the present committee system and the present allocation of power to committee chairmen. They argued that the Senate was not designed for majority rule. An undemocratic allocation of power, therefore, produced no distortion.

A: The object of the Senate is not to operate on a majority opinion. This is not the way the Senate was set up, nor was it the reason that it was constituted originally. It was for the exact opposite reason. It was for the purpose of trying to give equal representation to small states, as well as to big states, and to make sure that the majority, as such, did not run the country.
B: This underlies much of what seems to be arbitrary or irrational.
C: The theory of the Senate is balanced representation rather than majority rule per se and all by itself. It is the concept of Senators as ambassadors from the states.

THE POWER AND POSITION OF RANKING MINORITY MEMBERS

The ranking minority member on a committee or subcommittee has the primary responsibility for making sure that the minority party is represented at hearings and at other crucial points in the legislative process. This is sometimes difficult, particularly because at present there are only five or six Republicans on some of the major committees. This means the ranking member often performs most of the work himself.

The ranking minority member also has some prerogatives. If the committee provides for minority staff members he will be able to name all or most of them. The ranking members of subcommittees, if they maintain good relations with the chairmen, are able to exert considerable influence on the precise working of bills reported to the full committee.

The ranking members of committees also have power over minority party subcommittee assignments. The Republican round table participants testified, however, that for the most part the ranking Republicans followed seniority in assigning Republicans to subcommittees. This way they avoided intraparty disputes on the committee. A ranking member on a standing committee said, "I assign the minority members and the chairman respects my selections. It so happens that we work it out so that each member of the minority gets at least one subcommittee to his liking and this year it worked out that everybody got the subcommittee he wanted." Some senior Republicans are willing to waive seniority on specific subcommittees to improve the reelection chances of their colleagues.

The Republican senators indicated that there had been no serious problems with arbitrary ranking members being consistently unfair in their subcommittee appointments. The ranking members can, however, change the complexion of the minority side of a subcommittee by asking senior men to request specific assignments in order to take them away from heretical juniors. One Republican participant had this experience on a subcommittee dealing with immigration, a matter on which he differed with the ranking Republican:

I was put on the immigration subcommittee at one time, though I didn't rate it through seniority. Then somebody counted noses and it was suggested to me very tactfully that maybe I ought to step aside, which

I did, because I couldn't sustain the point on the basis of seniority. And I did it, too, because I didn't think it would gain me anything to contest with the party leadership in a matter of this kind, nor would it help the cause of immigration because they will simply add others to the committee.

Another Republican argued that the minority party was circumspect about subcommittee assignments: ranking members were not arbitrary and junior members were not pushy. "I think you have to recognize that the Senate is a matter of personal relationships. You just can't charge around like a bull in a china shop, demanding your rights like a member of the American Civil Liberties Union. You can do it, but you don't get anywhere that way."

The substantive task of minority members of committees is unclear. Since 1961, the task of the majority members of most committees has been clear: to take what the President and executive departments propose as the basic Democratic program and make what changes seem necessary in it before passing it. But there is no single minority party source of programs to support or amend. Naturally, the minority can always choose to support what the majority proposes. But, since the minority must constantly seek issues designed to win seats in elections, it will undoubtedly want to oppose a number of the majority proposals. Thus the minority faces the basic choice of merely opposing the majority or of offering its own alternatives.

A few ranking minority members try to lead in developing unified Republican positions. A junior Republican described the style of one ranking man:

He is one of the few that I know who takes the opportunity and the responsibility of getting the minority members together to decide whether or not we can have some kind of a position on a particular piece of legislation. I was absolutely delighted when this happened, because when I was in the House, I went to my ranking people on the committee and said, "Look, before we take a vote in committee, can't we for heaven's sakes get together and find out what we are doing, before we start?" I think this is imperative, and it is something we need very badly in the

Republican party. Otherwise, no one knows what anybody is trying to do or why they are trying to do it. But you just don't get that guidance from most senior members.

Most ranking Republicans, however, do little or nothing to bring Republican senators to a unified position on important pending business.

Some committees and the business they handle do not lend themselves to partisan maneuvering. Even on those committees that do handle partisan questions there may be great differences in ideology between the ranking Republican and some of the other Republicans on the committee. This makes the development of a unified party position almost impossible.

Junior Republicans who want to be active in the Senate are frustrated by the lack of activity on the part of the ranking minority members. Some senior Republicans agreed that more activity would be a worthy goal. At the same time that a new set of Republican leaders in the House was trying earnestly to activate the committee contingents to formulate Republican alternatives to major Democratic bills, the Senate Republican party persisted in the old pattern. Republicans, for the most part, could not expect leadership from their ranking committee members.

CONFERENCE COMMITTEES

Generally the chairmen and ranking minority members of committees or subcommittees lead the Senate into conference with the House. Their power is great at this critical point in the legislative process, but it is not absolute. The identity of the other Senate conferees varies from committee to committee. On some committees, such as Finance (which has no subcommittees), the same senior members go to all conferences.[9] On others, such as Appropriations, Banking and Currency, and Public Works, the senior members of the subcommittee from which the bill came are ordinarily appointed as conferees. Committee practice is particularly open to change when a new chairman takes office.

Practice also varies in the weight accorded the views of the individual conferees. Subcommittee chairmen who lead conference delegations generally determine the Senate position in conference alone, primarily because they know much more about the substance of the bill than any of the other Senate conferees.

Republican senators were bothered by the expectation that conferees have to uphold the position of the Senate. If the Republicans had fought a bill at every stage they felt that they still ought to have some leeway to reach advantageous compromises in conference. A senior Republican indicated that the longer a conference runs the more chance there is for individual senators with partially dissenting views to have an impact:

It is my impression that conferences always start out with all senators of both parties supporting the Senate's position. But if the conference drags on, the individual attitudes of the various members begin to show. Particularly if there is strong support in the other body for your position and against the Senate position, and something has got to give somewhere. Then you begin to put pressure on your Senate colleagues to give in to the House because that was the position you had on the bill in the first place.

The Senate often adds amendments to bills on the floor in order to provide room for bargaining with the House in conference. For example, one Democrat said, "On Appropriations you always appropriate above the House figure in the knowledge that you are going to cut it in half."[10] Other Democrats indicated the same kind of bargaining was planned on authorization bills for various programs.

Skillful floor managers can accept an amendment on the Senate floor and say, "We will take it to conference," when they really mean to sacrifice it in conference. Senator Russell Long, Louisiana Democrat and floor manager of the $11 billion tax reduction bill in 1964, used this technique often and skillfully. For example, he agreed to an amendment offered by Abraham Ribicoff, Connecticut Democrat, that allowed corporations a tax credit on the purchase of air- and water-pollution control equipment. This amendment was dropped in conference, apparently without serious objection by Long. On the Senate floor he had warned Ribicoff that he was not going to be a staunch defender of the amendment in conference:

This matter was discussed on a different basis in the committee. At that time the proposal would have had a much greater revenue impact. The committee could not agree to it. We have had an opportunity to examine the amendment of the Senator from Connecticut, as modified, with a much lower revenue estimate involved, and we will be glad to take it to conference and see what the House thinks about the amendment. Perhaps the House might not be willing to agree to it. . . . we are in no position to guarantee what the attitude of the House will be.[11]

A Republican, Kenneth Keating of New York, was aware of Long's general attitude toward taking matters to conference: "I hope that the words 'taken to conference' do not have a sinister connotation and that it will emerge from conference as well as being taken there."[12]

SUMMARY

In summary, the most senior members of the Senate committees, especially the chairmen, possess a great deal of power over substantive outcomes. The norms of Senate life are such, however, that most chairmen do not develop their potential power fully. They have come to be content with a situation in which virtually all of the majority members and at least some of the minority members of their committees possess a sizable amount of influence over legislative results. Senate norms neither force them to become complete democrats nor allow them to become complete autocrats. As long as they do not try to centralize power radically, they are accorded considerable deference. Presently they are operating in an individualistic situation that they are unable or unwilling to challenge frontally.

Notes

[1] See Donald R. Matthews, *U.S. Senators and Their World* (University of North Carolina Press, 1960), chap. 7.

[2] On the Banking and Currency Committee see John Bibby and Roger Davidson, *On Capitol Hill* (Holt, Rinehart and Winston, 1967), chapter 5; John F. Bibby, "Committee Characteristics and Legislative Oversight of Administration," *Midwest Journal of Political Science,* Vol. 10 (February 1966), pp. 78-98; Lewis A. Froman, Jr., *The Congressional Process* (Little, Brown, 1967), pp. 180-181; and Ralph K. Huitt, "Congressional Organization and Operations in the Field of Money and Credit," in Commission on Money and Credit, *Fiscal and Debt Management Policies* (Prentice-Hall, 1963), pp. 459-460. The phrases "service chairman" and "minority and restraining," used in the text, are Bibby's.

[3] For information on the lack of White House consultation with Fulbright, see J. William Fulbright, *The Arrogance of Power* (Vintage, 1966), pp. 47-53. On Stennis see Meg Greenfield, "Uhuru Comes to the Senate," *Reporter,* September 23, 1965, p. 35.

[4] See Daniel M. Berman, *A Bill Becomes a Law* (Macmillan, 1966, 2nd ed.), pp. 37-38.

[5] See Bibby, "Committee Characteristics," p. 83.

[6] Meg Greenfield, "The Senior Senator Kennedy," *Reporter,* December 15, 1966, p. 22.

[7] See Roger H. Davidson, *Coalition-Building for Depressed Areas Bills: 1955-1965* (Bobbs-Merrill, 1966), Inter-University Case Program No. 103.

[8] *Wall Street Journal,* February 8, 1966.

[9] For the conservative impact of this practice in the Finance Committee, see Huitt, "Congressional Organization and Operations in the Field of Money and Credit," pp. 453-455.

[10] See Stephen Horn, *Unused Power: A Study of the Senate Committee on Appropriations* (forthcoming), for a contrary view.

[11] *Congressional Record,* Vol. 110, Pt. 2, 88th Cong., 2nd sess. (1964), p. 2373.

[12] *Ibid.,* p. 2206.

Chapter 6: The Committee System: The Place of the Individual Senators

Congress makes most of its legislative decisions in standing committees and subcommittees. The Senate, as presently organized, affords every member the chance to become an acknowledged and influential expert in a specific field, usually that handled by one of his subcommittees. Not everyone can be on Finance or Appropriations, but virtually every senator can be a subcommittee chairman or the ranking minority member of a subcommittee. Consequently, most senators accept the standing committee system as presently constituted and complain only about peripheral elements of the system. An investigation of some of the principal aspects of committee life—assignment, organization, internal operation, and floor management—discloses the great range of freedom and the great

131

potential for legislative power afforded each senator. Specific examples from the past few years confirm that the total impact of the committee system is to spread substantive power widely.

THE ASSIGNMENT PROCESS

Senators face a committee assignment process that can be both frustrating and satisfying. In the 1960's both parties spread choice assignments more widely than before, and most senators favored this development. Those few who agitate for basic changes in the Senate have generally been denied committee seats they want badly.

The Democrats

The Democratic senators who participated in the round table discussions agreed that no single factor determines the committee assignments an individual senator receives, and that there is no centrally controlled "system" for making sure that all committees have certain legislative or ideological biases.

The Steering Committee is supposed to be the decision-making body, but senators were not sure how much independent weight it has. Whether it ratifies choices made by others on grounds already determined before the Steering Committee meeting or whether it really exercises independent judgment was unclear to them. Some members of the Steering Committee find it convenient to justify their actions to disappointed individual senators by claiming that they must follow the wishes of the leadership. The Majority Leader, on the other hand, when questioned by a senator who did not get committee assignments he desired, replied, "Well, I voted for you, but I only have one vote."

Democratic senators seeking new committee assignments are frustrated because they can pin responsibility for their fate on no specific man or committee. Most of them, however, put resentment aside and work hard on the committees they have been given. Because they continue to accumulate seniority, they also have some ground to hope for assignment to the preferred committees in two more years.

The senators agreed that the Majority Leader has an important, if not commanding, voice in the committee selection process. Lyndon Johnson had more influence on committee assignments than his successor, Mike Mansfield. One method used by Johnson to influence committee assignments was to have the Secretary for the Majority, Robert Baker, give advice to senators, particularly freshmen. When Mansfield became Majority Leader in 1961, Baker retained his position and continued this phase of his activities until his resignation in 1963, but his relationship to Mansfield was far different from his relationship to Johnson. Some senators felt he was operating on his own, or at least in response to important Democrats other than the Majority Leader. Baker's successor does not give this kind of advice.

One senator described Baker's influence on committee assignments for freshmen senators under Johnson:

Bobby is the one you asked how things went and where you went and who you talked to, and he said, "There is no chance of Appropriations; just forget that." He said the same about Foreign Relations. He said, "Don't mention that, at all, but look around and list any others you want," and then he made a few suggestions. As it came out, three other members of the class went directly on Appropriations in their freshman year, but I had been kept off.

The ignorance of freshmen rendered them especially susceptible to Baker's influence:

When you come in as a freshman, you just flounder around. My colleagues wouldn't even tell me the time of day, and I didn't have the slightest idea how to proceed, what the committees were, or anything else.

Chairmen vary widely in the amount of influence they wield in the assignment process. One senator with long service felt that only the chairmen of Appropriations and Finance were in a position to negotiate with the Steering Committee. Another Senator felt that all chairmen "can exercise a veto very effectively and I know it has been done, because I have had some of them tell me." The chairman of a minor committee said, "I have never indicated any choice. I have about three or four I would love to get rid of. I surely didn't ask to get them on there, I will tell you that."

The Majority Leader, Steering Committee, and committee chairmen take account of seniority, region, and personal preferences in picking committees. They also take into consideration the nature of the business coming before the committee in relation to the interests of the states whose senators are applying for membership.

Seniority is only a rough guide to Democratic committee assignments. Since the 1953 institution of the "Johnson Rule," which spread choice assignments to junior senators, Democrats have been more free to ignore seniority than before.

Region is clearly an important consideration. Most of the committees have Democrats from all sections. Geography dictates an imbalance on a few committees. For example, in 1967, ten of the eleven Democrats on the Interior and Insular Affairs Committee were westerners.

Most of the Democratic participants rejected the notion that the senior southerners conspired to control all committee assignments. But a few observed that the southerners ceded certain committees, such as Public Works, Labor and Public Welfare, and Banking and Currency, to the liberal Democrats so that the southern conservatives could concentrate their own waning numbers on the most important committees.

Several senators stated their belief that some specific group—the leadership, or the senior chairmen, or perhaps the Steering Committee—had a plan for controlling the most important committees, thus guaranteeing certain legislative results. Others believed that decisions were made more on the basis of personality than of desired ideological complexion.

Some senators insisted that private interests, especially producer interests, had a great deal to do with the complexion of committees.

One man said he had been subjected to "terrific pressure from the oil industry to quit Appropriations and go on Finance" (the committee that guards the depletion allowance). "They may have had sufficient strength to have me seriously considered, I don't know."

Some committees were identified as being particularly close to various producer interests. One senator described the Agriculture Committee: "I never think who is on the Agriculture Committee. I think of it in crops, and I think right where they sit at the table. We start with rice, cotton, sugar, tobacco, peanuts, broilers, and then you have a little wheat in there."

A member of the Commerce Committee referred to its membership in the same way: "You can count the number of people who are going to vote for the truck lines because the trucking industry is the major transportation facility in their state. The people who have a lot of railroad employment are going to be there to block any carriage of first class mail by air, for example."

Most senators favored this situation because they felt that competition between interests resulted in compromises that were generally good for the country. Said one, "When you put them all together you have looked after your entire society." Most senators are highly motivated to protect the producer interests in their states. Several agreed, however, that serving the interests of one's state does not mean simply accepting the definition of those interests offered by interest groups themselves. The individual senator also can define what is good for his state in relation to what is good for the nation as a whole.

Some senators work diligently to acquire specific assignments; others do not. Said one, "I worked like crazy to get on Appropriations. It took me about six years to get on that." A more complacent type indicated that he always responded affirmatively to leadership requests that he change committees: "I am just as well satisfied with one place as the other. I have no great desire to be on Appropriations. I would rather get along with the folks on Appropriations than be on it myself."

Most Democrats felt that it was important for a senator to get on his first-choice committee early in his career so he could start building seniority. But a few felt willing to adapt and develop seniority and power wherever they happened to land. Said one:

I asked for four committees. The first three I thought were crucial, and I am not yet on any of those first three committees. But I am getting a great deal of satisfaction from the committees I ended up on, and I think they are useful to my constituents and useful to me in terms of intellectual satisfaction.

Some of the Democratic participants felt that more justice would be done to individuals if the Steering Committee operation, with its vague responsibility, were scrapped in favor of an assignment committee on which every member had definite responsibility for promoting candidacies from a certain geographical area. Among House Democrats, who have such a committee, "there is always somebody on that committee you can talk to if you want an assignment real badly. In the Senate you don't know who in the hell to talk to. It is like spaghetti. You can't pick it up."

The Republicans

In theory the Republicans assign their members to committees solely by seniority. The man who has served in the Senate for the longest continuous time can claim any vacancy that occurs. If he does not exercise his option, the next senior man can claim it, and so on. For purposes of committee assignments there is a complicated formula that prevents any two Republicans from having equal seniority. In theory, the Republican Committee on Committees does nothing but ratify the automatic workings of seniority.

Despite the pressure of decreasing numbers in the Senate, which severely limits the number of seats on the choice committees, there have been changes in Republican practice. Now there is also some room for the leaders and the committees to exercise a brokerage function.

Republicans changed their assignment practices in 1959 and 1965. In 1959, with sharply reduced numbers returning to the Senate after the 1958 elections, junior Republicans keenly felt the lack of choice seats open to them. One of the Republican senators described the accommodation that was made:

The seniority system got too oppressive for some of the senators and there was a good deal of agitation among the Republicans. The senior Republicans, one by one, gave up one of their major committees to make room for the junior Republicans, and I recall how the pressure finally got down to one senator. He finally gave up one of his committees too. This was a change of climate, a change of atmosphere, rather than a formal ruling, but it became a custom which had considerable force.

In 1965 the Republican Conference made a formal change. Except for members already sitting, no Republican can now hold seats on more than one of the four most important committees: Foreign Relations, Appropriations, Finance, and Armed Services. A Republican now serving on one of these cannot fill a vacancy on another one, unless no other Republican wants it. Even with the changes of 1959 and 1965, seniority is still theoretically inviolable in every other case. Yet the floor leader and the Committee on Committees have a good deal of leverage in determining assignments.

The floor leader designates the chairman of the Committee on Committees, and this choice is approved by the full conference. The leader, after consulting with his chief lieutenants, then appoints the other members of the Committee on Committees. In the Eighty-ninth Congress this committee contained eleven of the thirty-two Republicans. All freshmen and others who want new committees submit their requests. If problems arise, the committee consults with the leaders, after which the committee submits the entire assignment list to the conference for routine approval.

Certain situations give the leaders a brokerage function to perform. For example, when Senator Strom Thurmond of South Carolina became a Republican, he had already served ten years in the Senate as a Democrat. The question was whether he should be placed as the most junior Republican on committees or whether his previous Senate service should have some weight. The leaders used the conference to discuss the problem. Finally, the members agreed to an arrangement whereby Thurmond would become third ranking (out of five) on Armed Services and third ranking (out of four) on Banking and Currency. But the formalities of the arrangement were such that the seniority system remained unaltered.

The leaders coax junior Republicans onto unpopular committees. One senator who most decidedly did not want a seat on Banking and Currency was put there by Senator Dirksen, the Minority Leader:

I just got raging mad. I went to Senator Dirksen and said I just would not accept it, and if he was going to insist on it, that I would be delighted to resign. We had a Republican governor, and he could appoint someone else in my place. I wouldn't do it. He looked at me with a great, broad grin on his face and said, "Would it make any difference to you to know that for the first time in history you have also been appointed to the Interior Committee, where your colleague is already sitting as a member?" That took the wind completely out of my sails, and I had nothing more to say, and accepted what was given to me.

Another point of entry for leadership influence develops if there is a contest that cannot be resolved amicably. Then the leaders may seek a more senior Republican to claim the opening in order to prevent any hard feelings between two junior members. Or, more rarely, if a Republican unacceptable to the leaders applies for an important committee post, they may seek to persuade a more senior Republican to apply for it in order to prevent him from getting it.

All of the participants—both "liberal" and "conservative"—felt that the seniority system, with its 1965 limitation, was the most satisfactory way to determine committee memberships. One liberal senator called it "protection for a person who might be in some danger of being discriminated against for any extraneous reason. This, of course, includes protection of the deviate from the norm of Republican doctrine, or the majority view among the Republicans. It has value as protection for the unusual guy." Another said, "If you do away with the seniority system, you simply could not have a campaign put on for committee positions. You would have everybody in the Senate owing somebody else something, and you would have a less honest Senate than you get by the seniority system."

ORGANIZATION OF COMMITTEES: SUBCOMMITTEES AND LEGISLATIVE SPECIALIZATION

The increased number of subcommittees has overextended most senators. Said one Democrat, in describing a typical situation, "I find myself much of the time with as many as three committee meetings going on at the same time." One Republican estimated that all senators had six to ten subcommittees each. Another Republican stated that he sat on two major committees, a minor committee, a select committee, and had memberships on fourteen subcommittees. A Democrat testified that he was on "about fifteen" subcommittees, and chaired three of them. He added, "For the last month I have been on three different subcommittees of Government Operations, all of which have been meeting every day at the same time." Another Democrat indicated that the problem was particularly severe on the Appropriations Committee, where each member might be assigned to as many as five subcommittees.

The senators perceived their plight accurately. In the Eighty-eighth Congress (1963-1965), each senator had an average of 2.81 full committee assignments, 9.19 subcommittee assignments, and 1.07 assignments to joint committees (evenly divided between full committees and subcommittees). Including conference committee assignments and board or commission assignments, each senator had an average of 19.49 assignments. A quarter of the members had 26 or more assignments.[1]

Members of both parties were worried about the proliferation of subcommittees. Some blamed it on the press of business coming before the Senate. A Republican blamed it on the "empire-building" desires of Democrats, but allowed that if the Republicans became the majority they would fall prey to the same instincts. Said another Republican:

I think we have too many subcommittees. That started some years ago, after the LaFollette-Monroney Bill passed. It began to deteriorate as soon as it passed, because every member of the majority party wanted to be important. It helps him get re-elected. Many subcommittees have been set up for the purpose of giving a chairmanship to a member of the majority party, to make him very important around home. Of course, it does help the ranking member of the minority party, too. They make the most of it, naturally.

Another development creating additional assignments has been the expansion of the size of committees. Table XIX summarizes the growth of some committees since the Reorganization Act of 1946 took effect.

One result of the proliferation of assignments is poor attendance at meetings. Consequently, a few senators make the decisions for any given committee or subcommittee. As one Democrat put it, "The senators actually physically present write the legislation."

TABLE XIX: SIZE OF SELECTED SENATE COMMITTEES, 1947-1967

COMMITTEE	NUMBER OF MEMBERS						Net change 1947-67
	1947	1951	1955	1959	1963	1967	
Appropriations	21	21	23	27	27	26	+5
Armed Services	13	13	15	17	17	18	+5
Banking and Currency	13	13	15	15	15	14	+1
Commerce	13	13	15	17	17	18	+5
Finance	13	13	15	17	17	17	+4
Foreign Relations	13	13	15	17	17	19	+6
Judiciary	13	13	15	15	15	16	+3
Labor and Public Welfare	13	13	13	15	15	16	+3
Public Works	13	13	13	15	17	16	+3

Another result is that senators do not keep up with the matters coming before many of their committees and subcommittees. If a senator is not present at a committee meeting there is little likelihood that he will read what happened in the record of the meeting. Most find it impossible to have a staff member cover all of the missed meetings. Some committees will not allow staff members at executive sessions. Neither will they allow staff members at meetings dealing with classified materials.

Staff members are sometimes too busy to go even to some of the meetings open to them. Committee staff can also be used by individual senators, but both junior Democrats and most Republicans felt that they had less access to committee staff than the senior Democrats and perhaps the ranking Republicans.

A third result is that senators concentrate on what interests them most among their committee and subcommittee assignments.

The participants had a few general suggestions for ameliorating this situation that forces a senator to ignore matters for which he is, in part, responsible. Several senators suggested that more staff —both personal and committee—might help. Some talked wistfully of having fewer assignments. Some favor reducing the size of committees because they feel that additional members make deliberations lengthy and circuitous.

Republicans thought that they had overcome some of the worst aspects of overassignment by spreading out the ranking memberships on subcommittees among all members. As one of them said, "This helps very much, because it provides a focus of interest for one of the fellows coming in, where he can really work on it. It also relieves the ranking member of trying to be an expert on every subject within that committee's jurisdiction."

The large number of committee and subcommittee assignments frustrates individual senators because of the excessive demands on their time. On the other hand, since each senator has a number of choices of subject matter on which he can concentrate, this makes it easier for him to weigh the relevant factors in deciding how to distribute his energies. On balance, the satisfaction of being able to make this choice is likely to outweigh the inconvenience of an overly demanding schedule.

THE INTERNAL OPERATIONS OF COMMITTEES

Division of Labor

Only a few senators are usually involved in making a committee decision on a substantive matter. Senior senators are generally more effective, even if not more active, than junior senators. However, the senior senators also delegate important work to the junior senators. Said one Democratic staff member, "There is a great residue of power in the Senate. The senators at the top have so much to do that if the younger senators can find a horse to ride the senior senators will generally let them, just because they don't have time to take it on themselves."

Another staff member described how a senior Democrat organized his committee in the 1950's when he first became chairman. "He had eight Democrats and seven Republicans. He arbitrarily divided the committee work into eight pieces. It was not because he was a good fellow but because he didn't want to do it himself, primarily. And they all worked." Dividing the work here stimulated activity, of necessity, on the part of even the most junior Democrats.

Interest is also important in determining which senators do the work. Said one staff member, "Legislation is really handled informally in a member's office with two or three of the most interested people there. Going into a subcommittee executive session is *pro forma.*" Interested junior senators can be extremely important in given legislative areas.

Some tolerance from senior members, interest, and the desires of the administration all worked together in 1966 to put Senator Edmund Muskie, Maine Democrat, in charge of the model cities bill in the Senate, even though he was only sixth ranking on the Banking and Currency Committee. His position on the bill prevailed both in the committee and on the floor. In a Senate strongly attached to a decentralized pattern of power distribution (to the committee chairmen) this probably could not have happened. But in a Senate characterized by an individualistic distribution of power, it was not unusual.[2]

Staff members are also involved at almost every point in the division of labor inside committees and subcommittees. Different patterns of work division prevail in various committees and they have legislative consequences. The Finance Committee, for example, under chairman Harry Byrd (1955-1965), had no subcommittees and virtually no professional staff. Much of the substantive work was done either by the staff of the Joint Committee on Internal Revenue Taxation, the staff of individual members of the Finance Committee, the senators themselves, or was perhaps left to the members and staff of the House Ways and Means Committee. One partial result of this situation was that the Finance Committee typically was in a weak position in substantive arguments with the House Ways and Means Committee. Another result was that the hold of the conservatives on tax policy was strengthened because liberal members of Finance had no access to staff and conservatives could rely on Colin Stam, chief staff man for the Joint Committee on Internal Revenue Taxation, to support their position with a variety of data.[3]

The Commerce Committee has standing subcommittees, although the full committee is the decision-making locus on many important matters. But, according to a staff member, "Individual members conduct the hearings and almost all Democratic senators have held some hearings. Commerce has such broad jurisdiction there is a little bit in there for everyone and a number of the members have a pet project and ride it through the full committee."

At another extreme stands the Judiciary Committee, which makes most of its decisions in subcommittees—some headed by extremely junior members—and the Appropriations Committee, which also makes most of its decisions at the subcommittee level—all headed by extremely senior members.

Republican staff members stressed the hard work done by senators themselves. They also stressed the influence of senior senators and the disproportionate amount of work done by them. The senior men of both parties on the various appropriations subcommittees are especially hard working and cooperative: [4]

It is the chairman of the subcommittee and the ranking minority member who do the great majority of the hard work and the hard thinking and have posted 95 percent attendance. For instance, the most complicated bill is Independent Offices Appropriations. The chairman and ranking man work completely together. The chairman trusts the ranking man to hold hearings by himself. He would never start a meeting without the ranking minority man, unless the Republican staff member present indicated it would be all right. They will never work at cross purposes. They finally get to depend on each other because it is a hard job.

The same kind of majority-minority compatibility exists on other committees. On one committee, according to a Republican staff member, "There is a tradition of having the subcommittee executive sessions more like seminars than strict party-line debates or fights."

The Republican staff members agreed with the Democrats that the senior senators are willing to delegate much of the work and some of the responsibility to junior senators. The ranking Republican on a committee typically will try to give every Republican at least one ranking position on a subcommittee that he wants. Thus, with interest already present, the Republicans will get more complete coverage of the work of the committee. Junior Republican senators gain trust and respect from their seniors if they work hard on their subcommittees. Also, the necessities of having representation on all subcommittees with only five or six Republicans on a full committee means that even a fairly junior Republican becomes "senior" quickly. One Republican senator who took office in 1961, for example, had by 1965 become a member of four committees and eight subcommittees, and was ranking Republican on three of the subcommittees.

Senior senators may prefer to share influence on important decisions with staff members rather than junior senators. Said one Republican staff member:

The staff man knows enough about his thinking and position so that he can represent his senior senator. A junior member of a committee owes a certain amount of allegiance to his ranking minority man, but that allegiance isn't as direct and strong and objective as is the allegiance of the staff man to his ranking senator. It would help to have more of the junior men learn more quickly how to take hold of the operating procedure and how to operate effectively and be a help. But there is a certain area in which no matter what the abilities and capacities of the junior members of the committee are, they are not going to satisfy the need of that overworked senior Republican senator. Only he can do it or his staff man.

Staff members help to "educate" junior senators; however, the fact that there are few freshmen in the typical Senate "class" reduces the opportunity for group cohesion and education. Senior senators do not volunteer information on how to be a senator. They are usually too busy and are not sure that they should do it. Also, junior senators who get committee and subcommittee assignments they do not want will often neglect those slots to concentrate on those that do interest them. Thus they may never become important or effective on most of their committees.

The position of the junior senator, then, is ambiguous. He can, with hard work and the right mixture of issues and personalities, become important on a committee or subcommittee in a relatively short period of time. But he can also be frustrated if he does not like the committee or the ranking man.

The frustration can extend even to a senator who has been in the Senate for a number of years but has just received a new assignment on an important committee. Said one Republican staff member:

Don't you think most junior members who are on Appropriations really are quite frustrated? They know they are going into an operation where two guys decide everything, the chairman and the ranking minority member. Really only one or two are ever there at the subcommittee hearing sessions, so if you ask a question really you are not going to have much impact on the future of the bill.

Another Republican staffer disagreed:

A junior man who doesn't get the subcommittee of his choice a lot of times is an unhappy fellow, so he doesn't participate. In fact we might not even see him for the whole session at the subcommittee. But if he does have an interest or just wants to apply himself, he could come to the hearing and have just as much or more time asking questions and developing the record as the next man. It is the members who develop the record and if a very junior member comes in and develops something in the record and shows some expertise, he will have some real influence in the subcommittee mark-up and in the full committee mark-up.

Staff members also gain their influence by working hard on the committees and subcommittees. One man stated that in his view the Democratic staff did most of the hard work on Appropriations. He also indicated that senators are so busy that in some committees and subcommittees the senator will depend on staff members to make important decisions for him. "I have often felt extremely uncomfortable because I am not responsible to the people of my senator's state, and to the nation—the senator is. Yet, I have had to make decisions no staff man should be called upon to make."

Partisanship

The degree of partisanship varies radically from committee to committee. Its appearance can be predicted on the basis of the issue at stake and the personalities of the important members of the committee. No committees always split along party lines. Most committees have a tradition of minimizing partisan considerations whenever possible. This style of operation helps individual senators enhance their personal power.

A Democrat offered one reason for a studied lack of partisanship on most committees: "You lean over backwards to try to achieve harmony, because you have to buck the whole Senate on a bill and if you can have the minority side with you, you have eliminated 90 percent of the opposition from the floor. If Republicans start after you on the floor, you have captive Republicans already on your side." Thus, for example, Senator Edmund Muskie, Maine Democrat, has always endeavored to keep bipartisan support for the bills reported by his Subcommittee on Air and Water Pollution. In 1963, the unity of Democrats and Republicans on the subcommittee helped diminish the impact of Republican grumbling on the floor.[5] In 1964, Administration Democrats on the Finance Committee were especially happy to have the support of two of the five Republicans on the committee for the $11 billion tax cut for the same reasons. One of the two whose support they successfully solicited was Minority Leader Dirksen.

A Republican staff member suggested another reason why overt partisanship is not a continuing phenomenon in most committees.

It must be remembered that when a man is elected to the Senate he has the right to ask for membership on the committees he would like to serve on. It is assumed that he has a personal reason or personal knowledge of information that that committee handles, the legislation that committee handles. So for that reason, a lot of times he places his personal reasons for being on that committee ahead of a party, or liberal or conservative reasoning that might apply to the legislation.

The Appropriations Committee, for example, almost never becomes involved in partisan argument. Thus power is channeled to individuals, not party groups. A Republican staff man described the operations of one Appropriations subcommittee:

I want to give you some kind of a feel for the lack of partisan feeling and the comradeship and the knowledge and experience gained by the ranking Democrat and Republican. Before we go into the subcommittee mark-up, the chairman and the ranking minority man will plan to get together. Just before they do that, the staff Republican man and the staff Democratic man will get together and they will define what the bad issues are and tell each other to go back to their senators and say, "Will you do this if we do that," and kind of talk around. Then the two staff men sit down with the chairman and the ranking minority man and have it out in private a day before the subcommittee meets. They pretty much have it worked out. When the subcommittee comes in and sits down they are faced with the two men who have gone through all the hearings, have pretty good first-hand knowledge and can speak in some depth on subjects under review.

Partisan splits occur on a few predictable issues that are handled by a few committees. Said one Democrat:

When it comes down to real basic issues, committees get partisan. Public power is one of the things. [Interior and Insular Affairs Committee]. Price supports is another. [Agriculture and Forestry Committee]. Over on the Finance Committee, interest rates is another thing that is concerned. There is a great range on Public Works. But I think that is, and should be, a pretty partisan group when it comes down to basic issues. Aid to Education [Labor and Public Welfare]. Resource development in National Parks [Interior and Insular Affairs]. Housing, on the Banking Committee. On every committee we can give an example.

A Republican staff member pointed to reclamation [Interior], Rural Electrification [Agriculture], and the money bills for agriculture and public works [Appropriations] as examples of bills that arouse partisan disputes.

Senators of both parties pointed to the Bobby Baker investigation as an issue that mobilized violent partisanship in an ordinarily calm and quiet committee, Rules and Administration.

Some committees have ideological splits that conform closely to party lines; others cross them. A Republican senator discussed the Commerce Committee:

You have, in Magnuson, as chairman, a real broker. He knows about how far he can go. He has a pretty good conception of the balance, which he maintains, between the railroad interests, the trucking interests, the canal interests, and all the rest of it. I don't think now of a single issue or fight there that was really a partisan matter.

But splits along interest lines do not prevent close cooperation in the work of the committee. The chairman and ranking Republican on

Commerce work well with one another. Another man familiar with the same committee said, "The Commerce Committee is almost unique in the extent to which it is 'government by consensus.' If a hot one comes up, the members of both parties will sit around and say, 'How in the hell are we going to get off this spot,' and they will stall. They will all write a secretary of a department and have him study the matter."

The style of individual chairmen also helps determine the presence or absence of partisanship. Said one Republican staff member talking about the Commerce Committee, "If Magnuson were defeated or resigned and the next man became chairman, it would become a very partisan operation." A Democratic staff member made the same point about the Banking and Currency Committee: "If we shifted from Fulbright to Robertson to Sparkman to Proxmire as chairman, I think the same committee would be very differently run in each case."

FLOOR MANAGEMENT OF LEGISLATION

Most committees have a high degree of success on the floor. The round table participants estimated that at least 90 percent of all legislation reported from committees went through on the floor with no trouble, and virtually unamended. Most senators "trust the committee." [6] In effect, this means that the one or two senators who typically make substantive decisions inside committees and subcommittees are making decisions for the entire Senate. Power is distributed individualistically because virtually every senator is the most powerful member of his party on at least one subcommittee.

Democratic staff members maintained that all committees are about equally successful in getting their legislation passed by the Senate, even though some chairmen are more effective in debate than others. They said that the Majority Leader would not allow a committee to bring a bill that had any chance of losing on the floor. When Eisenhower was President, the Democratic majority in the

Senate occasionally passed bills likely to be vetoed, but this was for the purpose of sharpening election issues.

Committees also appeared to the round table participants to be about equally successful in avoiding amendments on the floor. As one man irreverently put it, "I think I could take a hairy ape out to manage a bill and he could ward off amendments." Potential disagreements can usually be negotiated so as to avoid conflict on the floor.

Despite the general record of success on the part of all committees, the degree of skill on the part of the floor manager can affect the outcome. Said one Democratic staffer, "There are a few senators who stand up and offer amendments or handle a bill who make my boss say, 'Oh, God, why did he support it? That just cost me twelve votes.'" Another man described the most successful kind of floor manager:

[He] can make a vote for them look like something it isn't. Senator Kerr [Oklahoma Democrat] was the best I ever saw. He could make a vote for oil companies look like a vote for gas users. He built a major waterway up into Oklahoma and had it charged against Arkansas.

The Democratic staff members identified two major factors accounting for the success of almost all committees and committee managers on the floor. First, Senate floor procedure leaves a great deal of room for negotiation on the spot. Thus, potential defections can be prevented by wise negotiating. "You can suggest the absence of a quorum and you can negotiate your problems and by the time you come back in you have resolved your differences."

Second, the great use of unanimous consent agreements on the floor—even for important bills—facilitates committee success. This makes victory almost assured on most bills.

The Republican staff members had a different picture of the relative success of the various committees on the Senate floor. They differentiated between committees and assigned reasons for greater or lesser degrees of success.

First, the personality of the floor manager himself is an important factor. For example, "There is not a Democrat on the Senate Banking and Currency Committee who could handle the Housing bill on the Senate floor successfully other than Senator Sparkman. With Senator Sparkman managing the bill on the floor it has always been a success." Another chairman was identified as an unsuccessful floor manager—one likely to lose important amendments—because "He rubs everybody the wrong way and he can't really give a little to negotiate. I think his colleagues view him as having intellectual arrogance and sort of sneering down his nose at them and they don't like it."

Second, the subject matter at issue is important. Committees handling controversial issues automatically run a greater risk of having a major amendment they do not favor adopted on the floor than do committees handling noncontroversial issues. The Public Works Committee was cited as having a successful record on the floor because its bills gave "pork" to almost everyone.

Third, the degree of unity within the committee is important in determining whether the Senate will unquestioningly accept the committee's product on the floor. One man used the Appropriations Committee as an example:

Floor success is sometimes a question of the cohesion you have managed to develop within the committee. Without cohesion you would have utter chaos in some of our appropriations bills. We will just try to settle this in full committee and we have two or three senators who know what they will do but the rest of the committee will hold together. When you start off with twenty-seven members holding together, you have a good nucleus right there. That is part of management, too, and it is not something one man can take credit for. It just works that way.

Others spoke of committees, such as Finance and Armed Services, in which dissenters in the committee would support the committee on the floor. As one man remarked, "This is the ultimate of the committee system." At the other end of the spectrum are committees, such as Labor and Public Welfare and Interior and Insular Affairs, that bring their ideological and partisan splits to the floor.

The Republican staff members agreed with the Democrats that staff work is important in enabling a committee floor manager to know ahead of time what amendments to expect and what negotiations may be necessary. They also identified the ploy of "taking it to conference" as something that a skillful floor manager could use to avoid a defeat. An unskillful manager, however, can sometimes inadvertently accept something that the House conferees will also accept.

INDIVIDUAL SENATORS AND THE PRESENT COMMITTEE SYSTEM

From the individual senator's point of view the balance sheet on the committee system at present is extremely favorable. Most senators may find minor annoyances in the system, but principally they find great satisfaction in it because of the opportunities the system affords them for developing both institutional and personal power.

The assignment process can be annoying because of the vague location of responsibility for assignment decisions. If a senator does not get the assignments he thinks are due him, especially if he is a Democrat, he does not really know who to blame. But most senators get at least some assignments that please them, and both parties now have rules governing the assigning process that distribute the choice seats widely.

Once on his committees the individual senator may get subcommittee assignments that do not give him a chance to work on the subject matter that really interests him. But, given the large number of subcommittee assignments he receives (an average of over nine), he is likely to find one or two congenial subcommittees that handle matters in which he rapidly can become expert. Each individual senator is quickly thrust into a subcommittee position in which he becomes the leading expert for the entire Senate. Then he is in a position to exercise power alone—or with the aid of a few staff members and perhaps with the agreement of one senator from the other party. The decisions thus made are almost always accepted by the entire Senate.

That the system allows virtually everyone to participate can be shown by a number of examples. The examples also make the point that it is easier for majority party members to participate fully than it is for minority party members.

That chairmen have substantive influence has already been shown. Other senior members who have not acceded to the top position on a committee also have substantive power. Long before he became chairman of Banking and Currency, John Sparkman, Alabama Democrat, made the important decisions on housing for the Senate. Even the presence of an unsympathetic chairman of the full committee did not lessen his power.[7]

Men late in their first term can develop immense power. For example, Senator Muskie became the leading government figure on air and water pollution in his fifth year in the Senate. He also became one of the leading figures on intergovernmental relations at the same time.[8] Mike Monroney, Oklahoma Democrat, became the leading congressional spokesman on civil aviation in his fifth year in the Senate and retained that position for fourteen years.[9]

Senators in their first few years also develop substantive impact rapidly. Birch Bayh, Indiana Democrat, piloted a constitutional amendment on presidential succession through the Senate in his third year in the Senate. In his first year in the Senate, Joseph Tydings, Maryland Democrat, served as chairman of a subcommittee on Improvements in Judicial Machinery. Edward Kennedy, Massachusetts Democrat, served as chairman of the Subcommittee on Immigration and Naturalization early in his first term. He and Gaylord Nelson, Wisconsin Democrat, fathered the teacher corps bill after only a few years' service.[10] In his first year in the Senate, Harrison Williams, New Jersey Democrat, became the chief promoter of mass transit legislation. He retained initiative in this field and after six years of sustained effort saw the bill become law in 1964.[11]

Even senators who are "mavericks" on many matters can become influential on important matters and can acquire important chairmanships. After nine years as an "outsider," William Proxmire, Wisconsin Democrat, became chairman of the Joint Economic Committee and chairman of the Subcommittee on Financial Institutions of the Banking and Currency Committee. In the first position he has expanded the impact of the committee on fiscal policy making. In the second position he has become the chief sponsor and promoter of truth-in-lending legislation.[12]

Minority members, including the most junior, are also accorded some deference on substantive matters. For example, in his first year in the Senate, Charles Percy, Illinois Republican, seized a leading role in the housing field.[13]

The present committee system, then, can be visualized as a large collection of individually important positions—typically subcommittee chairmanships and ranking minority memberships on subcommittees. The most important of these positions are reserved for the most senior members of both parties. But those of lesser importance relatively are still extremely important absolutely and are, in effect, reserved for the senators of middle-level and junior standing. General participation of all senators in this system is not only allowed, but encouraged. There are few senators who are excluded for long or completely. The power of all senators is maximized in most committees by the practice of delegating work to subcommittees. Staff members of committees and of individual senators also participate in this distribution of power, although more unevenly than the senators.

Notes

[1] These data are in Appendix A of *Organization of Congress*, S. Rept. 1414, 89th Cong., 2nd sess. (1966).

[2] On Muskie and the Model Cities bill see Martin Nolan, "Muskie of Maine," *Reporter*, July 13, 1967, pp. 45-46.

[3] See John F. Manley, "The House Committee on Ways and Means: 1947-

1966," (Ph.D. dissertation, Syracuse University, 1967), chapter 5. Since Russell Long has become chairman of Finance in 1965 and since Colin Stam retired in 1964, some changes have taken place that may alter this situation. Six professional staff members were added to the one professional already employed by Finance. Laurence Woodworth, Stam's successor, is more willing to serve all members of Finance (and House Ways and Means) and not just the conservatives.

4 For the very different (unfavorable) view of the Senate Appropriations Committee held by the House Appropriations Committee members. see Richard F. Fenno, Jr., *The Power of the Purse* (Little, Brown, 1966), pp. 100-101.

5 See Randall B. Ripley, "Congress Supports Clean Air, 1963," in Frederic N. Cleaveland (ed.), *Congress and Urban Problems* (Brookings, 1969).

6 Occasionally, however, the Senate gets in a mood to reject the work of a committee, either completely or through a series of amendments that completely change the intent of the committee bill. For an example of the latter case, see the discussion of the Senate's excise tax amendments to the tax bill in 1964 in Manley, "House Committee on Ways and Means," chapter 5.

7 John F. Bibby, "Committee Characteristics and Legislative Oversight of Administration," *Midwest Journal of Political Science*, Vol. 10 (February 1966), p. 85.

8 See Ripley, "Clean Air"; and Nolan, "Muskie of Maine."

9 See Randall B. Ripley, "Congress Champions Aid to Airports, 1958-59," in Cleaveland, *Urban Problems;* and Emmette Redford, *Congress Passes the Federal Aviation Act of 1958* (Bobbs-Merrill, n.d.), Inter-University Case Program No. 62.

10 On Kennedy see Meg Greenfield, "The Senior Senator Kennedy," *Reporter,* December 15, 1966, pp. 19-24.

11 See Royce Hanson, "Congress Catches the Subway: Urban Mass Transit Legislation, 1960-1964," in Cleaveland, *Urban Problems.*

12 See the article by Norman C. Miller in the *Wall Street Journal,* June 30, 1967.

13 See the column by Joseph Kraft in the *Washington Post,* January 20, 1967.

The Consequences
of Dispersed Power

Chapter 7: The Nature of the Legislative Process in the Senate

Neither party leaders nor the chairmen of standing committees control the legislative process in the present Senate. They play important, but far from dominant, roles. Individual senators possess much legislative power if they can successfully cope with the vast number of nonlegislative demands on their time. Senators delegate part of their legislative power to staff members. Staff members acquire additional power in part through their own efforts and in part by default on the part of the senators.

The central features of the legislative process in the present Senate include a high degree of specialization by individual senators in areas usually coinciding with a few of their subcommittee assignments, a scarcity of reliable broad-gauged information on procedure, intentions of others, and substance, and an omnipresent attitude that mutual helpfulness is the key to accomplishing anything and the indispensable quality of a "good senator." Given the absence of a single consistently dominant force in the Senate, legislative action takes place, usually in sporadic bursts, only when a single senator or a small group of senators decide that a winning coalition has been formed that will support a proposed action. Not only must individual senators await these developments before their ideas pass the Senate in bill form, but outsiders, including the President, must await the same developments before their ideas earn an affirmative response from the Senate.

The present individualistic distribution of power results in a segmented legislative process in which there is no consistently dependable central element that can guarantee a steady flow of outcomes or determine the nature of those outcomes. A constant formation of coalitions for and against specific legislative actions marks Senate activity. No single coalition remains in existence for long and none is a reliable winner on more than one or a few issues.

The nature and impact of specialization has already been discussed. The tendency it produces is for each senator to concentrate on his own area or areas of expertise. He expects his opinion to be respected in these areas; and he respects the opinions of other experts in other areas. Deliberation on substance is typically restricted to the "experts." Communication on substance is minimal.

The rest of this chapter will explore other aspects of the individualized distribution of power that lead to the segmented, sporadic legislative process in the present Senate.

THE PROBLEM OF INFORMATION

Senators need a continual flow of relevant, accurate, and up-to-date information about substance, procedure, and the intentions of other participants in the legislative process if they want to achieve some measure of legislative effectiveness. Yet in the present individualized Senate most senators can obtain such information only in connection with the one or two subject matter areas in which they are most highly specialized. This information allows them to maintain some control over events in those areas, but in other areas they are likely to be uninformed and, therefore, impotent. As was pointed out in Chapters 4 and 5, neither the party leaders nor the committee chairmen at present regularly have access to enough information to put them in a position of controlling a broad range of matters.

There are five primary sources of information for members of both parties. First, a senator can rely on himself. Long hours of studying a subject can make a senator into a reliable and fairly complete repository of relevant information on a narrow topic. Said one Democrat, "The complexity and the multiplicity of the legislative problems are such that you tend to concentrate in some areas in which you become a considerable expert." Another said:

I have devoted half of my legislative career to education bills. I think I could sit down and analyze an education bill and work it out myself. I have done a little work on taxes, but mostly I would rely on the committee staff, or some expert on that. On some areas such as armed services, or where you are going to put a plant, I have no conception or idea. I rely completely on some other member of Congress.

A Republican made the same point:

I rely on my own study and my own experience in hearings on banking problems. But when I work on the Medicare bill I have to rely on other Republican senators who are on the committee, on reading, and on some visits with lobbyists.

Other senators, who also have developed substantive specialties, comprise a second source of information on legislative matters. Said one Democrat:

Usually I start with a position—whether on health care or consumer legislation or the budget or something else. Then I am looking for material to substantiate my position. But I don't take a positive stand on something like Vietnam—which I don't know much about. Then I am inclined to listen to Fulbright [Chairman of the Foreign Relations Committee]. You have to have faith in somebody. You listen to them in those areas.

The third primary source of legislative information is staff. Some senators put great reliance on their personal staffs, while others use them only on constituent matters and speech-writing and rely on committee staff for information on legislation. Some send their personal staff to committee meetings, when it is allowed, if they cannot attend themselves. Others rely on committee staff or on their own reading to brief them on missed meetings. Almost no reliance is placed on the legislative reference service of the Library of Congress.

Fourth, interest groups are an important source of information. Genuinely useful information from this quarter usually comes in response to specific senatorial requests and not from the routine lobbying efforts of the groups themselves.

The Administration is a fifth primary source of information, especially for the members of the President's party. Said a Democrat, "If an Administration bill is sent down to us, it has a lot of weight before it ever gets to committee." Added another, "The normal channel for information, if you are not in one of your own expert areas, is to go first to the department that is concerned. If you want to delve still deeper than their report, you ask them to come up and give you a briefing." Republicans are generally less impressed with information from the Administration, but still pay some attention to it, especially if they have no reliable sources of information providing a contradictory set of facts or suggested solution.

Senators of both parties agreed that it is much easier to gain information about matters coming before their own committees than about matters coming before other committees.

Republicans said that if the junior Republicans on a committee had ideological differences with the ranking committee member they could not always look to him or the minority staff for reliable information. Among Democrats, ideological differences did not appear to play such an inhibiting role in the flow of reliable information within committees.

Democratic senators were content with the information they had for purposes of legislating. They were most concerned about the business of their committees and subcommittees; the information they received on this business struck them as adequate. They were, however, discontent with the amount and quality of information on the floor schedule—an inadequacy for which they blamed Majority Leader Mansfield.

Republican senators, because of their minority status, ran into more problems in getting the information necessary for making informed legislative judgments. They thought their knowledge of the scheduling of business for the floor was adequate, but maintained that the majority party was less than generous to them in many committees. They were aggrieved by the lack of adequate minority staff. Additional unhappiness was expressed over the paucity of information provided by the majority on committee scheduling and committee business. Said one Republican of his committee experience,

The majority does not notify the minority of the pendency of hearings until the last minute; they don't give the minority the opportunity to see projected drafts of reports and recommendations and don't advise the minority until the night before, or sometimes until the actual time of the hearing of those who are to appear and testify. The majority does not give us the information which is a necessary element in our being able to prepare ourselves as well as they do.

The Republicans also believed the use of security classification by the Administration prevented the acquisition of information that they needed. They saw the need for security classifications, but suspected that the Administration was often using them to cover mistakes.

MUTUAL HELPFULNESS AND LEGISLATIVE EFFECTIVENESS

Personal qualities help determine whether a senator will or will not be effective legislatively. The most effective are the most admired; admiration leads to influence on substantive matters. The personal qualities most esteemed are helpfulness and thoughtfulness. Senators who build credits by being helpful to their colleagues and thoughtful of them can expect them to reciprocate. Ideology retains some importance in that it provides certain bounds beyond which senators will not go in the desire to help each other. Party affiliation provides considerably weaker limits.

The Effective Senator

The Senate is an intensely personal place. The senators and staff members of both parties at the round tables agreed that the men with the qualities most admired and respected—given at least some philosophical compatibility or an absence of ideological hostility—will be the most influential. If one senator perceives in another senator qualities of which he approves, he may consequently tend to trust the legislative wisdom of the second senator. Senators and staff members define legislative effectiveness in terms of such intangibles, not in numbers of bills sponsored or passed.

Two Democratic senators discussed this point:

A: Effectiveness is a question of how much a senator is listened to when he speaks on a piece of legislation.

B: There are people in the Senate that you can talk to and not be sure that anyone else in the Senate will follow them. They are not the leaders of any little group. To be effective you have to be identified as a spokesman for a certain policy or a certain program. There are people you rely upon in their various committees and in their various activities.

A: I think there is some fall-out from this, too. If you learn to respect a senator in his particular speciality, if he doesn't speak too much and speaks thoughtfully, you are going to respect him, even when he is outside his speciality.

B: Even when he could be wrong.

A: That is right. It builds his credibility. Other things being equal, you tend to follow him. There is a certain loyalty built around class, too. The class of '58, for example. We lean over backwards to support each other.

Fellows you get to know and like and respect are fellows you are going to be receptive to, on whatever question they discuss. No matter whether he is a Republican, a Democrat, a southerner, or a northerner. Members of your committees are people you learn to know best, and this is a very important association. It is harder to say no to a friend than to a stranger. These human relationships I think are very important.
B: I think they are tremendously important.

Younger senators can establish themselves as "comers" if they learn to appear thoughtful and even deferential at the right moments. Senator Edmund Muskie, for example, in skillfully managing the model cities bill in 1966 "made no attempt to embarrass his opponents or to suggest that they were either heartless or thoughtless about the nation's cities." The commentator added, accurately, that "deferential diplomacy is money in the bank for a senator who seeks a position of leadership." [1]

Senator Edward Kennedy has been able to develop substantial legislative influence inside the Senate because he, too, has been thoughtful of his elders. For example, in conducting floor debate on his poll-tax amendment to the 1965 voting rights bill, he was "amiable and restrained when the Southerners—whose pride in their reputation as Constitutional lawyers often exceeds their mastery of the law—attacked him as a callow interloper. And even though the outcome was touch and go . . . Kennedy resisted every temptation to score points by humiliating Majority Leader Mike Mansfield, who was charged with defending the bill against the Kennedy amendment. Mansfield, who is not himself a lawyer, was evidently out of his depth in the legal debate." [2]

Kennedy showed similar qualities of thoughtfulness when he deliberately stayed in the background in his attempts to pass both the Teacher Corps and gun control legislation. He let others get the publicity. He deferred to the Foreign Relations Committee on the problem of Vietnamese refugees, although he had been working on it in his Judiciary subcommittee. [3]

Republican senators agreed that there were no tangible, quantifiable measures that could be applied to senators to determine their degree of influence.

A: I think it is completely intangible. I don't·think there is any tangible measure. None of us know how many bills who got through, do we? None of us pay attention to it.

B: That isn't the way you keep score. It is the general judgment of the legislator, whether or not he knows what he is talking about, whether he is tolerant of the opinion of others, whether he is successful in being persuasive, whether he is fair and decent in his dealings with his colleagues. Those are the standards. That is why a man like Senator Byrd [the late Harry F. Byrd, Sr., Virginia Democrat] stands so white-marble-high in the Senate's estimation.

C: Senator Russell, I think, is another one usually kicked around a little in the press as being the leader against civil rights but he has enormous respect in the Senate.

B: His word is good. He won't take petty advantage. He will tell you the truth.

A: Where do you get the feel for the strong men in a fraternity, or in any other group of men? I think it arises the same way in the Senate. A combination of respect for his attitude and his ability and your personal relations with him.

B: We can think of senators who are very new, in a year or two, who are already regarded with approbation and great respect, but they have as yet no legislative success. But they are men who are already marked as men who have the respect of their colleagues.

The Republicans felt that it is no more difficult for a member of the minority party to gain stature in the Senate than it is for a member of the majority. This feeling compensates Republicans somewhat for the frustrations of being in the minority:

A: I don't think it is any harder for a minority man to earn this status of respect than it is for a Democrat. We all pretty well judge our colleagues the same, and I imagine if you could get rid of the ideological factor, and then ask the senators to rank their colleagues, I think there might be a similarity in the rating. But, of course, you can't get rid of the ideological factor—and to a few people Harry Byrd is a devil with horns.

B: I would say that it might be easier in the minority party as a new member to gain respect within the minority party than it is for a new member to gain respect in the majority party, solely on the basis of size. But I wouldn't dispute the judgment that on an overall Senate basis, I don't think it makes much difference. I think your colleagues judge you as a person, and not necessarily on whether they agree with your views or not.

Minority members can be especially effective if they cultivate friendships with important figures in the majority party. Among the reasons for the substantial influence of George Aiken, Vermont Republican, for example, is his close friendship with Majority Leader Mansfield.[4]

Staff members of both parties agreed that attractive personal qualities, coupled with hard work, are necessary for the development of legislative effectiveness and influence.

One Democratic staff member stressed the importance of substantive competence: "How does the senator develop effectiveness as a legislator? Stay at work. He must know what the legislation is, what it does, what the history of it is and what it means when it is implemented."

Staff members cited Senator Russell of Georgia as the best example of a man who is effective because he is universally respected:

A: He plays a good game and is easy to get along with.
B: He is a bright man.
A: He has conservative views, but understands other senators. He plays the game in committee. He is not difficult, and he has seniority. I think almost every senator will swear by certain things about Senator Russell.
B: When you mention Richard Russell most people turn to the Rules fight and civil rights and they don't realize his standing with his colleagues and his effectiveness in space, atomic energy and national defense.
C: Also, he had his other standings for twenty years before anybody even heard of the Civil Rights bill. He had a huge standing before that even became an issue.
B: The Senate is the most exclusive gentlemen's club in the world. Just think of the qualities that make up a gentleman and you can understand effectiveness.

A reporter made the same point about Russell in somewhat more tangible terms: "In his long service he has had no colleague who is not in his debt for help and for a personal consideration embellished by an exquisite courtesy." [5]

The Republican staff members held essentially the same views. Their primary stress was on hard work and personal "accommodation":

A: The ones who are effective have to do their homework. Otherwise, they are not taken seriously.

B: I think effective senators must have a spirit of accommodation, too. You can work hard but if you haven't a spirit of accommodation you won't succeed.

C: You have to have a certain amount of personal relations. I can think of some senators on our side who work extremely hard, some young ones. If this one senator I have in mind had an assistant who had the guts to pull him down into his seat when he got up to nit-pick on bills, he would really go much further than he is going to go.

B: One of the people they most fear getting up and offering an amendment is John Sherman Cooper [Kentucky Republican]. It has been said that the definition of a gentleman is someone who refrains from inflicting pain wherever possible. I think that is a quality that Cooper has that makes him almost a bipartisan-type character. If Cooper has a fairly decent amendment, even in this Senate, [which was Democratic by 67 to 33], he can go in and pick up forty to forty-five and sometimes carry it.

The Ineffective Senator

Most senators at the present possess enough attractive personal traits to help them develop at least some legislative effectiveness. However, a few, six to ten according to their colleagues, possess traits that reduce their influence to almost nothing.

Three Democratic senators discussed this phenomenon:

A: There are senators who stand on the floor and offer an amendment, and you just vote against it when you find out the name of the senator who offered the amendment.

B: The first one that was pointed out to me when I came here was Senator Y. Automatically anything he is for, everybody is against.
C: He has come up too often with too many nit-picking amendments; fellows who back hopeless causes all the time are also impotent legislatively.
B: Would you say that every time they support a hopeless cause, they damage themselves?
C: Not a single cause—but if they develop a habit.

The Republican senators pinpointed certain personal traits as the cause of ineffectiveness:

A: There are a few little rules of thumb. I think my colleagues would agree with me that a senator who talks all the time forfeits considerable respect, regardless of his party. He forfeits influence. When you are talking all the time, you aren't thinking, and you aren't allowing room for a few other people to express their thoughts. It is a domineering and dominating thing. Also, senators know well enough that nobody can be an expert on every subject under the sun. Even the press ignores that sort of a person after a while.
B: It is a manifestation of a combination of selfishness and arrogance, and people despise that.
A: I think selfishness is a trait very much resented in the Senate.

Democratic staff members agreed that arrogance and talkativeness diminish a senator's legislative effectiveness:

A: If a man commits himself, if he talks on every issue, I think he is regarded with some suspicion by his colleagues. I think you have to pick and choose.
B: Senator Z speaks on everything at the drop of a hat. He offers six amendments on any bill pending.
C: I notice on the Senate floor there is a degree of reaction to individuals on the basis of when they say things, how they say it, who they are.
B: Senator Z offers amendments on the floor which he never bothers to offer in subcommittee or committee. The reaction to him is adverse. He makes his fights on the floor when the press from his state is watching. By this kind of action, oftentimes a senator can become ineffective.
C: That is right. And he whines. When he comes over to talk about it before he does it, he whines about it.

A Republican staff member summed up the views of all round table participants: "Ungentlemanly conduct" leads to legislative ineffectiveness:

There is a code of propriety. Senators Aiken and Prouty were up in Vermont for a function they could not avoid, and this joker offered an amendment to cut Vermont's proportion of highway aid. That was bad enough with both of them being absent, and when Senator Dirksen explained that they were necessarily absent, this guy insisted on pressing for a roll call vote and finally Mansfield and Dirksen and Kuchel and everybody jumped on him and very reluctantly and cursing like hell, he went in the cloakroom and withdrew the amendment. Now that is ungentlemanly conduct that you just can't get by with.

LEGISLATIVE INITIATIVE AND SUPPORT

An examination of senators initiating and gathering support for legislative ideas reveals the impact of specialization, limited information, and the tie between effectiveness and personal traits on the legislative process. Its segmented, sporadic nature becomes outstandingly apparent.

Legislative Initiative

SUBJECTS FOR INITIATION. A senator's committee and subcommittee assignments determine most of the subjects on which he will introduce bills about which he is serious. As one junior Democrat put it:

The big thing is the luck of the draw on committees. My big campaign push was water pollution and air pollution. I put in for the Committee on Public Works but was not fortunate enough to be assigned to it. So, although I am tremendously interested and I am a strong proponent, as far as my being able to specialize in that field, it is just out of the question. On the other hand, I was fortunate enough to be put on the Judiciary Committee, and I didn't even ask for it. And on the Judiciary Committee we are going to handle reapportionment, where I am going to be able to take a role. Also I am able to be active on voting rights.

A senior Republican said:

I don't know how often a man just reaches out in the blue and gets a legislative idea and tries to buck it through. It is much easier if you do have a proposed bill that comes into your own committee where you can do something about it. I have discovered that many of my good ideas that went to some other committee just went there and died.

Another Republican disclosed that his main interests lay outside the committees on which he served, but that he bent his interests to fit the committees while still hoping for assignment to the committee of his first choice some time in the future:

My main interest as an individual, rather than as a senator, is in foreign affairs. But I am still nowhere near senior enough to be on the Foreign Relations Committee. I am restricted to a degree by my committees, and therefore my interests are the type that interest my state: transportation problems and industrial and employment problems in the Commerce Committee and problems which interest our lawyers and our legislators in the Judiciary Committee.

Added another Republican:

You can become an expert in whatever field your committee is sovereign and people listen to you and rely on you for information and judgment and all kinds of things, even though it may not be your primary field of interest.

Because subcommittees legislate, in effect, for the whole Senate, a subcommittee assignment not only gives an individual senator an opportunity to specialize but puts pressure on him to do so.

The great time pressures on individual senators mean that only one or two men are likely to make the decisions on a given subcommittee. Thus a senator who chooses to specialize in the subject matter handled by a particular subcommittee can, in effect, speak for the Senate on that limited part of the legislative spectrum. One Senator estimated that there were really only about twenty working weeks in a year—taking off weekends, holidays, and recesses—during which a senator could pay much attention to his committee work. Said he:

You split this time among your subcommittees and your other obligations, because unless you pay some attention to all of your subcommittees and your full committees, they are not going to pay much attention to your work, and if you want to get your bills out, you have to at least give their work a lick and a promise. The real problem is to find the kind of time that you can focus on a piece of legislation and really digest it and work it over. I attend a lot of committee sessions, of course, where I don't feel I really make a contribution.

This situation gives those senators willing to concentrate on the work of a subcommittee or two great power in those subcommittees. And it also forces them to concentrate on only one or two subjects if they want to develop influence. This produces a situation in which a large number of highly specialized experts generally accept each other's work without much criticism.

A few other factors help determine the fields in which an individual senator will initiate legislation. These include the problems of the state from which the senator comes and his own interests. But these factors are of minor importance compared to the impact of committee and subcommittee assignments.

SOURCES OF LEGISLATIVE IDEAS. Senators rely on their own knowledge of substantive matters and of particular state problems for many of their legislative ideas. They also rely on staff members. They may also rely on outside individuals or groups. Some will introduce legislation specifically labeled "by request"; others will not. Private immigration and claim problems are, of necessity, brought to the attention of the individual senator by the person seeking some specific kind of legislative relief. Senior members, especially committee chairmen, are more likely to receive requests to introduce general legislation. If a senator becomes publicly identified with a specialized area, he is likely to get requests to introduce legislation either from interest groups or from an executive agency.

Several Democrats testified that they would not introduce legislation by request unless they favored it or unless it had a specific impact on their state. They also admitted that if they got requests from insistent people they would usually put in a bill or co-sponsor someone else's bill but they would not work for its passage. Said one,

You never expect those bills to go anywhere. They are just a printed piece of paper to send out to constituents to mollify them. You introduce a bill and that is the end of it.

One Republican revealed less flexibility:

I have never put the words "by request" on a bill. If I didn't want to introduce it, I wouldn't introduce it, and if I did, I would stand up and put my name on it.

Another Republican declared that he would introduce legislation requested from the outside if he thought it helped solve a genuine problem.

There are forms of self-interest which mesh right into your own interests of trying to keep your people employed in the state. An illustration of that is that in my state some of the steel companies have asked me to introduce a bill—and I have done it—which would provide for impression into steel containers an indication of where they were made, whether in the United States or in a foreign country. I was glad to do this. Surely, it is a special interest group, but it is on a very high plane because it is designed to help them to stay in business and provide employment.

Democrats also named the Administration as a source of legislative ideas. But they stressed the cooperative aspects of what they did with the Administration. On the aid to education bill, for example, they attributed ideas both to the Administration and to interested members of both houses of Congress.

The Administration wanted an education bill, but I think most of the details of the bill were worked out in consultation with members of the Congress before it was introduced. It was satisfactory to us even before it was introduced, and that is how we got it through the Senate without an amendment. I am sure that the pattern is to work out the introduction of major legislation with the committee chairman involved, or the persons or the leaders principally concerned.

Another Senator asserted that the pattern varies from bill to bill, and that Congress plays a large and important role in many instances:

The Peace Corps, for instance, was brand new, and that was an Executive idea. But the Appalachia Bill originated in the Congress. People in the Senate and the House of Representatives wanted to work out something for the region. I think that that was a tripartite sort of thing.

One Democratic Senator offered a convincing statement that most legislative ideas originate in a cluster of individuals and interests surrounding each subcommittee.[6]

You generate some of your own legislative ideas out of your own natural interests and out of your committees. If you are a subcommittee chairman this means that you are going to get the assistance of staff, of the executive agencies over which the committee has supervision, and from the special groups which are concerned with the work of your committees. One of the great problems legislatively, it seems to me, for the Congress as a whole, is that increasingly legislation depends upon the quality of the work of a subcommittee. And that usually means one or two men. This may be good or it may be bad, but it is happening.

THE SPECIAL PROBLEM OF THE MINORITY PARTY. The principal Republican problem in initiating legislation is simply stated: the majority party members have the power in the Senate to apportion almost all of the credit for legislative ideas to themselves, and they usually do so. As one Republican Senator graphically put it:

This is like hunting truffles. The French farmer hunts truffles with a pig on a leash and when the pig reaches the truffle, the farmer hits him on the snout and takes the truffle. If you are interested in knowing you have gathered a lot of truffles, you can do it, but if you try to outsmart the farmer, you don't get any truffles at all.

Several Republicans elaborated:

A: In the present legislative situation no Republican bill has a chance to get passed, at least with a Republican name on it.

B: Since that is so, your best hope is to make a record, according to your specialties, or to secure what you regard as improvements in a bill through amendments, or to become known as a specialist in this field, which puts you in a relatively stronger position, should you later be in the majority.

C: I co-sponsor some bills with Democrats, but it is always called by the Democrat's name.

A: I have had an interesting experience on this. I have a junior colleague from my state who is a Democrat. After he was elected he moved in and claimed all of the bills that I had introduced in the past that affected our state. They appeared with his name on them, in the new session, and we had quite a tussle about it. He answered me very simply: "I can get them passed. As long as your name is on those bills, I can see that they don't pass. If you want the bills passed you have to surrender them to me."

B: That is what my Democratic colleague tells me in clear terms. There is only one way to get the credit, and that is by being a majority or being so close to the majority that they have to trade over the fence and give us some of the bills.

A: I still keep introducing bills. Occasionally, if they survive at all, they survive as an amendment to an Administration bill, and they disappear. You just have the satisfaction of knowing that you were able to change this particular bill, but your name disappears.

B: Often we introduce a bill which is just highjacked from us by a Democrat, but that leaves you free in your own state to go back and say, "A Democrat grabbed my bill. These are my ideas, and he got it passed, but the original work was done by me." You can get some people to listen to that.

Developing Legislative Support

The general stress on mutual aid that characterizes the Senate, particularly in committee, results in a great deal of bargaining and trading of credits. Trades of one specific item for another are not often made. But if a senator helps another senator, he anticipates that when he needs help at some future time he will be able to obtain it from the person he is presently helping. Most senators keep no detailed accounts on these trades, but a man soon establishes a reputation for being either helpful or unhelpful on legislative matters.

The pattern of generalized trading of good will or credits occurs in large part within the confines of the majority party on major legislative matters, but it does cross ideological and regional lines. For example, senior southern conservatives offer support to the rest of their party. Two liberal northern Democrats discussed a southern chairman:

A: Yes, he is helpful; he gave me two bills last year out of his committee. There is no *quid pro quo* stated by him.
B: It is just survival of the club. You have got to help each other out.

Senators are likely to be especially helpful to a colleague facing reelection. Two liberal Democrats discussed this phenomenon:

A: In that last two-year period, when you are up for reelection, your senior colleagues will be wonderfully cooperative.
B: There isn't any better argument for something than "I need it for reelection."
A: They will go out of their way to be helpful.
B: You can't work this on major legislation that is a matter of principle, but you can work it all the time on other things. For example, on the Interior Committee a subcommittee chairman stepped down so that a man running for reelection could have the job. Then this year, after he had won, the senior man took it back.

Mutual helpfulness and trading of credits also extends across party lines. The minority party may develop considerable influence if the help of some of its members is needed by the majority in order to pass bills.

A Democratic senator stressed the importance of mutual helpfulness as he described the kind of Republican most likely to receive Democratic help in passing bills:

There is cooperation in helping minority members with bills, especially in cases where the Republican is someone who has been very cooperative. It is not something going beyond your conscience or anything like this. Some of them are helpful, even though they are on the other side. In certain cases, you help them.

Without this kind of reciprocity few bills would get through the Senate's legislative process, which, in most instances, allows one or two strong opponents well-placed on a committee or subcommittee to prevent action. Furthermore, even in the absence of strong opponents, there are so many bills crying for attention that many die by inaction. Thus, if a senator wants a bill reported by a committee on which he does not sit and passed on the floor, he needs friends. One Democrat described what motivated him to be helpful in such a situation:

I have done some things on Agriculture because a specific individual Senator asked me to do it. I think if it was somebody else I never would have taken it up at all. But you do try to help somebody, because you like to. This man is a nice fellow. He is cooperative, and he will help you. You could take his bill or leave it, but you will go all out to help him pass a piece of legislation that he needs in his territory. People sometimes don't earn their right to be helped. Some people never help you on anything.

Another member added that when an amendment comes up in committee or on the floor the name of the sponsor is often all-important. If the sponsor is a "cooperator," his amendment has a good chance; if he is not, it is likely to be defeated automatically.

BARGAINING FOR LEGISLATIVE SUPPORT. Members of both parties are anxious to get the support of a number of allies as they seek to attain their legislative goals. In general, the more allies they can acquire, the better their chances of success. The typical relation between an individual senator and an ally is reciprocal. The senator needs his support at the moment, but there are numerous other times when the potential ally will need the aid of the senator.

Perhaps the most consistently necessary support for a senator of either party is that of the members of at least his own party on the standing committee handling a bill in which he is interested. Minority party members obviously need some help, at least in the form of benign apathy, from majority party members if they are to succeed. Minority party help, although not essential, can also make the path to success smoother for members of the majority party.

On some matters it is essential to have regional unity. A solid bloc of western senators, for example, can often make a demand involving reclamation and get results. These regional blocs are often bipartisan.

At times an ideological bloc is helpful in passing or defeating legislation. Detailed provisions of tax bills often involve an ideological confrontation. Typically, this kind of bloc is centered in one party, with a few allies from the other party.

It is well to have the support of the Administration or at least some piece of the executive branch. Sometimes a senator will seek White House or departmental support for something he is initiating. At other times he will help a department or agency with some matter in which it has special interest. Said one Democrat, "This is a two-way street, especially if you have established rapport with people in the Administration." Said another:

If the White House helps me get a bill of mine passed in the House, it is almost mandatory for me to do something in the Senate to help the White House.

Interest groups can be useful allies. Two Democrats discussed the reciprocal nature of this relationship:

A: We use lobbyists just as much as they use us. You gather together the people who are in favor of your position and send them trotting over to the House to generate some support. On all bills in which I have a major interest I call a meeting of the lobbyists and say, "How about it," and they go to work on congressmen and senators.
B: These lobbying organizations can do for us what they do for themselves. That is, they work through the grass roots of congressmen and senators.

Allies in the House of Representatives are essential if a bill is going to make its way to the President's desk. House members often need the same kind of aid from senators.

On some matters the support and interest of state and local officials can also be important.

A senator of either party can use three basic techniques as he seeks support from these various potential allies. First, he can seek to create a climate of mutual helpfulness that does not rely on explicit bargains (exchanges of tangible considerations) at the time. If a senator can, over time, convince a number of potential supporters— particularly other senators—that he is likely to cooperate with them when they need his help, they may extend support on the basis of that implicit bargain.

Such a climate can be developed within an entire party or at least among those members of a single party who are in a position to influence a given substantive decision. For example, in 1959 all Democrats in positions of influence, both liberals and conservatives, agreed on the content of the major labor bill of that year. They reached a mutually agreeable compromise because they realized that they all had more to gain than they would lose by such common action. Had the House Democrats been oriented the same way, the Democratic party could have avoided the acute embarrassment of seeing the Landrum-Griffin bill become law in a heavily Democratic Congress.

A climate of mutual helpfulness can also be developed within an ideological grouping that crosses party lines, although the center of gravity of such a grouping tends to be in one party. For example, in 1965, liberal Democrats took the lead in opposing Senator Dirksen's constitutional amendment that would have negated the Supreme Court's decision on reapportionment of state legislatures. But they also got vital Republican help: a key vote in the Judiciary Committee from Jacob Javits of New York that forced Dirksen to seek a two-thirds majority on the Senate floor rather than a simple majority, and three votes on the 57 to 39 roll call that left Dirksen seven votes short of the needed majority.[7]

General mutual helpfulness can also be established within single-party groups formed on some basis other than ideology. For example, early in the Ninetieth Congress (1967-1969) the six new Republican senators formed a study group. Most of these senators also happened to be young and more liberal than their elders. The club, formed to study national issues, received briefings from high-ranking officials. It is likely that the associations in this club helped establish a feeling of mutual helpfulness between the members that could have an impact on substantive matters.[8]

Bipartisan regional blocs can make legislative demands. A Western Democrat described his efforts to create such a bloc:

I spent a good deal of time this year trying to get six million dollars for the Bureau of Land Management, for soil erosion control, which is important to my state, and important to every other place in the West. Today they marked up the bill and we got the soil erosion control. That is one in which I personally appeared before the committee and wrote letters to every other western senator to try to get support.

The second basic bargaining technique that can be used by senators of both parties is the specific or explicit bargain, which may take a number of forms. It may involve a trade that will support either logically competing or mutually exclusive interests. In the mid-1950's, for example, Senator Paul Douglas, Illinois Democrat, began to work for legislation aimed at aiding depressed areas economically. He had no hope of success if only urban areas were included in the definition of "depressed areas." Thus, to attract support from senators from basically rural states he encouraged the addition of provisions making rural states eligible for the aid he proposed.[9] Similarly, when the cotton bill seemed in danger of failing in 1964, members of both parties in the Committee on Agriculture and Forestry cooperated in adding a wheat title to the bill. Thus two major agricultural interests (and the cotton manufacturing interests) were benefitted by the same bill, and it passed largely because of this union.[10]

Regional interests may also be involved in a specific trade. Two Democrats discussed the passage of the Appalachia bill in 1965 to make this point: [11]

A: It was born with the West Virginia Senators out of a long, persistent problem of high unemployment and the decline of their principal resource.

B: But they couldn't pass it as a West Virginia bill. They just didn't have enough help.

A: That is right; it became regional.

B: They stuck in a piece of North Carolina to get their help. In order to get help from both Republicans and Democrats they had to take in Kentucky. Olin Johnston said, "South Carolina will support that thing, but you put in the northwestern part of South Carolina," and he named the counties.

A: As you very well know, other regions of the country which had a high incidence of unemployment and economic problems had to be promised informally that there was something coming along akin to Appalachia in which they would have an opportunity to improve their condition.

Some explicit bargains are offered by the majority party as concessions to the minority party. In 1959, for example, the Democrats wanted to enact housing legislation, but they faced the possibility of a veto from President Eisenhower if their program cost too much. Thus they needed either to placate the White House by amending their proposals, or they needed to attract enough Republican votes in Congress to override a veto. After the Banking and Currency Committee had agreed on a program, Majority Leader Lyndon Johnson met twice with Eisenhower to talk about the bill. As a result, he offered amendments cutting $225 million from the program. His strategy did not work, since the President vetoed the bill and the Senate upheld the veto. On two subsequent bills the Democrats made even more concessions until finally the third one received almost unanimous Republican support and the President signed it.[12]

On other occasions a potential majority may need to offer specific concessions to a bipartisan ideological group in order to prevent possible defeat. In 1964, after liberal forces had narrowly defeated stringent "states' rights" amendments to the poverty bill, they acquiesced in two compromise amendments with milder provisions. They believed these concessions necessary to guarantee final passage.[13]

Specific trades between two key individuals may also be extremely important. These may be based on specific interests, regional needs, ideology, party loyalty, or just close friendship. In 1961, for example, Senator Douglas, in effect, made a personal trade with Senator J. William Fulbright, Arkansas Democrat. Douglas agreed to support Fulbright's amendment on the floor to put th administration of the new area redevelopment program in the Commerce rather than in a new independent agency; Fulbright was to support the bill as a whole. Thi several years of complete disagreement between two men over proposals for aid to depressed areas.[14]

In 1962, medicare failed in the Senate only because Senator Robert Kerr, Oklahoma Democrat, was able to persuade Senator Jennings Randolph, West Virginia Democrat, to vote against it. Kerr and Randolph were close personal friends. In addition, Kerr had assisted Randolph in obtaining provisions he wanted in the welfare bill, the bill to which medicare was being offered as an amendment. Randolph apparently did not want to jeopardize his place in Kerr's affections or the welfare provisions for which he had labored.[15]

The third technique that both Democrats and Republicans can use in seeking support is to anticipate opposition by seeking it out and compromising with it. The price of compromise may often be less if the opposition has not been expressed openly or publicly. One Democrat described his style of operating in this vein:

I think allies are easy to identify. It is just a question of alerting them and making sure they are on your side. The real problem is to pull the teeth of the opposition. I think the best way to do that is to make your committee hearings undertake an honest and thorough identification of the nature of the opposition, and try to counter it on the record. You meet it head-on. You counter it with other testimony and counter it by questions, by cross-examination, and then finally undertake to the extent that you can, without sacrificing principle or sacrificing your bill, to draw the teeth of the opposition by recognizing and meeting the grounds for the opposition.

You carefully try to remold your bill so that it can be as precise an instrument as possible for doing what you want it to do, without arousing unnecessary opposition. If you leave stuff in there that people can play with and make wild statements about, that is not necessary. If you don't need something that is such a red flag, then, for God's sake, get rid of it.

According to one close observer, Senator Edward Kennedy, Massachusetts Democrat, seeks legislative success through molding his along the same lines. His staff members are "under standing ons to keep themselves and him informed of the twists and turns his legislation takes in the House, whether the appropriators are of a mind to starve one of his projects, and/or what the administration is up to with a bill that has already become law. When a measure of his is in trouble, he will make the phone calls and pay the visits himself, exploring the best terms he can get. If the administration can't be prevailed upon to support a bill, can it at least be dissuaded from issuing an unfavorable report? If the amendment is unacceptable in its present form would this language or that solve the problem?" [16]

In guiding the passage of legislation on air and water pollution, Senator Edmund Muskie, Maine Democrat, has proved to be a master of ferreting out and silencing opposition before it becomes vocal.[17] In 1961, Harrison Williams, New Jersey Democrat, displayed great skill in meeting the technical objections of organized labor to the omission of certain provisions in the mass transit bill before the complaints became fatal to the success of the bill.[18]

THE SPECIAL POSITION OF THE MINORITY. The minority party member is usually in one of three positions as he strives to attain any legislative goals of his own. First, his chances of success are often dependent on attracting majority party support—either from senators or from some part of the executive branch or both. Two Republican senators discussed the possibility of success in attracting such support:

A: If you have the right kind of relationship with the Democratic chairman or a prominent Democrat on the committee that is going to hear your bill, you would like to talk to him. You have to get that kind of support. On one of my committees, where I am ranking Republican, I have the most effective cooperation from the chairman. I am not sure all the ranking Republicans have this kind of relationship.

On a committee on which I do not serve, I would go to someone on that committee about bills affecting my state and ask them to watch for them and do what they can.

B: Within limits, you can get a considerable degree of cooperation from the Democrats. For instance, I can go to the chairman of the two major committees on which I serve and I can at times persuade them to either hold hearings or to bring up a bill in which I am interested or to bring up a bill which has a chance of passage, in which case I pay the price of having a Democratic name on it. But they will do all those cooperative things, providing they don't run counter either to their own policy or the policy adopted by the Democratic Committee.

The Republican participants in the round tables remarked that typically they could get help from parts of the executive branch only on bills that had no political significance.

A second position in which a Republican may find himself permits him to extract a number of concessions from the majority party members because of circumstances that have made his support crucial to their ultimate success. For example, Senator Dirksen was able to insist on restrictions on immigration from the Western Hemisphere because his vote was absolutely essential to gaining a favorable report from the subcommittee of the Judiciary Committee handling the bill in 1965.[19]

Third, a minority party senator may be in a position to gain part of his legislative desires by truly cooperating with a key member or members of the majority party. For example, Frederick Payne, Maine Republican, sought to meet problems of his state and to make his own campaign for reelection less difficult in 1958 by cooperating with Douglas in pushing for depressed-areas legislation.[20] Since the formation of the Special Subcommittee on Air and Water Pollution in 1963, Caleb Boggs of Delaware, ranking Republican on it, has attained many of his legislative preferences through close cooperation with chairman Muskie.[21]

THE LEGISLATIVE LIFE OF A SENATOR

Virtually all senators can acquire substantial legislative influence. Those who do not have it usually have disqualified themselves by violating the Senate's code of acceptable conduct that is understood by most members. The code is not highly restrictive, and only repeated violations bring sanctions; the sometime violator may retain all or most of his influence. Only a few senators have ignored the code altogether and thus forfeited most of their legislative impact.[22]

The round table participants did not complain of the oppressiveness of the "system" or the excessive power of the "Club" or the "Establishment" or some other in-group. They did not resent the code of behavior they described, with its stress on cooperativeness and mutual helpfulness. Their chief satisfactions came from the legislative impact they felt they could have in committees and subcommittees.

Members of both parties were frustrated principally by the lack of time to do all they wanted to do and felt they should do on the numerous matters coming to their attention. Members of the minority party felt some additional frustration at being denied what they considered the proper credit for some of their legislative ideas.

The Senate is not composed of a few omnipotent and happy senior senators and a great many impotent and unhappy junior senators. Most senators are content with their lot. Most of them feel that they have a considerable amount of legislative potency, at least in selected fields. They are not sure there is a "Club," but if there is they are convinced that their membership will come to them automatically when they attain enough seniority. Meanwhile they are largely satisfied with life in the Senate.

Notes

[1] Martin Nolan, "Muskie of Maine," *Reporter*, July 13, 1967, p. 46.
[2] Meg Greenfield, "The Senior Senator Kennedy," *Reporter*, December 15, 1966, p. 20.

[3] *Ibid.*, p. 21.

[4] See the story by Dan Cordtz in the *Wall Street Journal,* March 3, 1966.

[5] Quotation is from the column by Doris Fleeson in the *Evening Star* (Washington), January 11, 1963.

[6] The senator is talking about what Ernest Griffith called "whirlpools." See Griffith, *Congress: Its Contemporary Role,* 3rd ed. (New York University Press, 1960).

[7] *Washington Post,* August 8, 1965; and Meg Greenfield, "Uhuru Comes to the Senate," *Reporter,* September 23, 1965.

[8] *Evening Star* (Washington), February 2, 1967.

[9] Roger H. Davidson, *Coalition-Building for Depressed Areas Bills: 1955-1965* (Bobbs-Merrill, 1966), Inter-University Case Program No. 103.

[10] See the 1964 *Congressional Quarterly Almanac,* pp. 103-107.

[11] For a more extensive and different picture of the origins of the Appalachia program see James L. Sundquist, *Politics and Policy* (Brookings, 1968).

[12] See Glen Gordon, *The Legislative Process and Divided Government* (University of Massachusetts Bureau of Government Research, 1966).

[13] 1964 *Congressional Quarterly Almanac,* p. 225.

[14] Davidson, *Depressed Areas Bills.*

[15] Eugene Feingold, *Medicare: Policy and Politics* (Chandler, 1966), pp. 123-124.

[16] Greenfield, "Kennedy," p. 22.

[17] See, for example, the discussion of his role in passing the Clean Air Act of 1963 in Randall B. Ripley, "Congress Supports Clean Air, 1963," in Frederic N. Cleaveland (ed.), *Congress and Urban Problems* (Brookings, 1969).

[18] See Royce Hanson, "Congress Catches the Subway: Urban Mass Transit Legislation, 1960-1964," in Cleaveland, *Congress and Urban Problems.*

[19] See the *Wall Street Journal,* October 4, 1965.

[20] Davidson, "Depressed Areas Bills."

[21] For a discussion of Boggs' role in the passage of the Clean Air Act of 1963 see Ripley, "Congress Supports Clean Air."

[22] For a view that the Senate no longer possesses a meaningful moral code (and for considerable weeping over the loss) see the column by William S. White in the *Washington Post,* December 18, 1967. For more persuasive views that a loose code still exists and that its most consistent violators lose influence see the stories on Senator Russell Long by Walter Mears in the *Evening Star* (Washington), December 15, 1967, and by Mary McGrory in the *Sunday Star* (Washington), December 17, 1967.

Chapter 8: **The Power of Staff**

There are only one hundred senators, but there is enough work in the Senate to keep at least two thousand other men and women busy.[1] They work as staff members for individual senators, committees, and subcommittees. Much of the work they do is routine— typing letters, answering relatively unimportant mail, chatting with constituents. But much of the work they do is also extremely important. Some of them perform sensitive political chores for individual senators. Many of them become intimately involved in the details of legislation. When senators cannot follow the deliberations on a bill because of competing demands on their time, staff members in effect make legislative decisions for senators.

The pattern of power distribution among senators at any given time helps to determine how much legislative power personal and committee staff members can develop. Changing facts about life in the Senate, such as the increasing availability of funds to hire staff members, also help determine the legislative impact that staff members can have.

Since the end of World War II, more staff members have acquired more legislative power than previously for a combination of reasons. The Senate has become increasingly involved in a larger and more complex range of business. This has opened new substantive specialties for staff members. At the same time, the number of staff members in the Senate has proliferated greatly—both on committees and in senatorial offices. Most important, the attitudes and perceptions of staff members and the attitudes and perceptions of senators have aided staff members to increase their legislative power. These attitudes and perceptions are closely related to the existence or development of an individualistic distribution of power.

At present, most top staff members—administrative or legislative assistants in individual senatorial offices and professional staff members for committees—actively desire and seek legislative power. They still must remain largely invisible and anonymous in relation to the outside world, but within the confines of the Capitol Hill community they are aware of the desirability of acting in ways designed to increase their influence.

Senators are ambivalent in their attitudes toward the power of staff members. On the one hand, most of them actively want more staff members, both in their own offices and responsible to them on their various committees and subcommittees. They want these men and women to be talented and dedicated. On the other hand, they are jealous of their power and usually reluctant to share it. They also have some worries about nonelected individuals performing the work of elected officials.

The conflict between the desires of the senators and staff members is partially resolved by selective perception on the part of both: they each see what they want to see. Senators realize that they delegate some legislative power to staff members because of the overwhelming press of business, but they usually maintain that they retain the final power of decision on all matters. Staff members see the world differently: they see themselves as making a number of final decisions for the senators. To be sure, they worry somewhat about getting too far from the senator's general wishes and preferences. A prolonged record of making decisions without senatorial concurrence might well lead to the necessity of seeking new employment. Staff members also worry about their lack of responsibility to the electorate. But these worries stop neither the desire for legislative power nor the necessity of exercising it.

PERSONAL STAFF

The Organization of Senatorial Offices

The guiding principle behind the organization of each senator's office is the personal style of the senator himself. He may wish all of his top assistants to report to him directly. He may want to see only some of them, either regularly or sporadically. Or he may want all staff communications channeled through a single top assistant.

Virtually all senatorial offices are organized functionally. Typically there are one or more professionals in charge of public relations, case work, legislation, political affairs, and office administration. The professionals are, of course, aided by a number of clerical employees. At least one office uses a substantive division of labor instead of the customary functional division. A Republican staff member described the two different patterns:

Senator X uses the subject-matter approach to staffing; we use a functional approach. In X's office the four top assistants are divided by subject matter. One would handle Civil Rights and he would handle the legislative side, the administrative side in terms of implementation, the press side in terms of press relations and releases, and the appropriations side. In our office this subject would go bouncing back and forth depending on the point in time between the administrative side and the legislative side. Someone deals with legislative problems; someone deals with administrative problems; someone handles the press; and someone handles political matters back home.

The central purpose of the pattern of organization adopted in every senatorial office is to routinize as much of the work as possible, thus leaving both the senator and the top staff people additional time to concentrate on legislative matters.

A Democratic senator explained the necessity for making as many matters as possible routine:

We are all handicapped with too few people and too little time, so what you try to do is get the routine down to the bottom of your staff, at the lowest level in your staff where it can be handled effectively, and to get as large a part of your workload in that category as possible, so that your top people are available for creative work—whether that involves your legislation in committees or your floor work, or projects for your state, or difficult political problems. What you have to try to do is narrow the area within which your talented people work and still cover all of the important policy-making and decision-making that needs to be done in your office.

Handling mail is particularly subject to efforts at routinization. Senators generally see only those letters containing something personal or posing a new problem. A senior Republican from a sparsely populated state outlined his mail procedure:

In handling the mail, we have a formula, a pattern worked out by which the mail that I am supposed to handle personally is sorted out, and the rest of it more or less all filters through the administrative assistant and as the letters are written and come back ready for mailing, my administrative assistant backstops me and reads every letter which I am to sign.

Division of responsibility among staff members is also aimed at routinization: Said one Republican:

My administrative assistant hires and fires the rest of the staff. He also runs the office. He assigns duties. He attends one of my committees, backstops me, and my legislative assistant handles the work pertaining to the rest of my committees. My administrative assistant sees many con-stituents—particularly business and labor groups. My legislative assistant sees the kind of people with legislative problems and also backstops me on the floor, keeps me advised of the progress of legislation in my com-mittees, and coordinates with other legislative assistants. He advises me about the pending amendments and votes occurring on the floor, and has generally heavy responsibilities. Then I have a public relations assistant. All three of these top men are backstopped by men with less experience. I am training a second team in case I lose any of this fairly expensive talent.

Most senators seek specialists who can handle highly technical matters rapidly and accurately without bothering the senator him-self. Said one Republican:

There are some areas of particular concern to my state where I have somebody on the staff who has his nose to the grindstone on that, all the time. My general office organization is very informal and is based in part on the personalities and capacities of the people who are on my staff. I have an administrative assistant, and it is his job to run the office, but he and I make the assignments. I try to keep one person handling problems that are peculiar to my state. I have a press secretary. I have two or three people to handle case work with downtown agencies. This is based on their backgrounds. Then I have one all-around staff man. I don't have a person who is designated as a legislative assistant. Rather I divide these duties up. We divide up all the committees on which I serve and those on which I do not serve too and assign them to someone. It is very in-formal and the assignments are constantly changing as people come and go. I try to take advantage of the particular ability or background of each individual on the staff.

A Democratic senator praised two of his staff members who were particularly adept at handling immigration and social security matters:

We have many, many Oriental cases—Japanese and Chinese who want to bring in families. Some of it I just don't even see, unless it comes to the point where they need a private bill. She handles it and is very sympathetic. Every Christmas she gets lace tablecloths from Hong Kong. I have a man on my staff who knows all the social security laws and ins and outs better than I do, and he handles all of these. Occasionally he will come to me with a case that is kind of persistent and stubborn.

Top staff members in senatorial offices complained that far too much of their time was taken up with the mail, the telephone, and visits by constituents. They saw life in a senator's office as a constant fight to get enough time to do something important. Said one Democrat:

There are many dissimilar things about senators' offices but there is one thing that is the concern of every senator's office. It is what we talk about when we get together—and that is the volume of work in any senator's office. It is staggering. In the last twelve months—and I have been here ten years—I have seen our mail volume double. I have seen in the last six months two additional telephone lines come into the office and our switchboard is still blocked. We can't get the big picture on legislation because we can't shake loose long enough to get it. We would like to.

Another long-time Democrat staff member made the same complaint:

Constituents gradually get to know that they can deal with you instead of the senator and this is why the longer you stay here the more you are chained to the telephone and to the desk.

Republican staff members, especially those from large states, found life no simpler than their Democratic counterparts. Said one from a large state:

Our senator gives us a free hand to do what we like. But part of what we do is by sheer necessity. When you have 1000 to 3000 letters a day, you have a lot of trash that you have to deal with whether you like it or not before you can ever get to the legislative area. That is why probably most of the decent legislation around here is done by senators from small states.

Said another large-state staff man:

We are besieged by constituents on the telephone wanting to come down at the drop of a hat to see the senator. We are flooded with mail—500 to 1000 letters a day and thirty percent of this is on legislation. I am the legislative assistant. I have another fellow working with me, but in a situation like this obviously you can't be an expert, you can't specialize in one area, you can't really sink your teeth into one subject that might interest you because if you do you let everything else fall by the wayside. And you are also kind of a lightening rod to take care of the swarms of people who come in or call you up.

The Legislative Impact of Personal Staff

Staff members in individual senatorial offices can and do have substantial legislative impact. Case literature provides ample evidence of such influence. For example, many of the specific agreements between the senators of both parties and between the subcommittee and interest group representatives—agreement that helped guarantee the success of the Clean Air Act of 1963 in the Senate—were made by four staff members. One of these men, a Democrat, was employed by the Public Works Committee. But the other three, a Democrat and two Republicans, worked for individual senators who were members of the subcommittee. They had the confidence of the senators and maintained it by checking some of their decisions with their principals before the time for final decision in the subcommittee arrived. They also reached agreements that received, of necessity, only cursory scrutiny from the senators before final ratification.[2]

A close study of Oklahoma Democrat Mike Monroney's staff concluded that it "is designed to play many of the roles of a United States senator with a minimum of personal intervention."[3] His staff concentrated on matters relating to Oklahoma and constituents and on speech-writing and public relations, but they also played a role in policy-making and legislating. One man, who worked for Oklahoma Democrat Robert Kerr before coming to Monroney's staff, was so effective on water resources and reclamation matters that he was referred to as "the third senator from Oklahoma." His main impact was focused on legislation and administrative actions that affected Oklahoma and the Southwest generally. On these matters he operated with the blessing and general knowledge of his senator, but he was also free to make a number of his own decisions as he proceeded. These decisions sometimes affected legislative outcomes.

In the development of the bargains and compromises that led to the passage of the Mass Transportation Act in 1964, Senator Harrison Williams' legislative assistant, Ardee Ames, played a partially independent role.[4]

Many senators, however, especially Democrats, indicated that their personal staff members were likely to be too busy to have much legislative impact. Said one Democrat:

Your personal office staff is not likely to generate much legislation. They are kept so damned busy with their nose to the grindstone answering constituent mail and trying to do a polished job of it. Your administrative assistant should be able to talk about legislation with you, but he is so busy taking care of people, trying to find out where to apply for a job under the Economic Opportunity Act, and all these other things, that he can't.

Data on the division of funds to pay for administrative staff and for legislative staff in senatorial offices gives some support for this view. For example, Senator Thomas Kuchel, California Republican, spends twice as much for staff members with essentially administrative duties as he does for those with essentially legislative duties.[5]

It is difficult for a senator to break his personal staff free for legislative duties, but efforts to do so can pay off. Said one Democrat:

If you have a guy as administrative assistant who has special skills in the legislative field then you try to use him there. My AA's time is limited, but he generates a hell of a lot of good legislative ideas in every one of my three subcommittee areas. Not to use that would be bad. So we try to organize the rest of the staff work so that the others pick up more of the routine load.

Republicans felt more strongly than the Democrats that their personal staff members were able to offer considerable aid on legislative matters. This perception is accurate and the situation is the product of necessity: many of the Democrats had some committee staff on which they could draw for legislative help. But only a few Republicans had any committee staff on which they could rely for the type of legislative aid they wanted. Several Republicans talked about the legislative role of their personal staff:

A: They are an important source of legislative ideas in the area of state-related legislation. I have staff specialists working particularly in the area of public lands, which is vital for my state.

B: I have told my legislative assistant and his assistant that I welcome their just trying ideas out on me in an informal memorandum. I will pick out several such memoranda and say, "Let's follow this through."

C: All of my legislative ideas are things that I have been working on and worrying about for an extended period of time, and trying to get through. I won't say my staff is not imaginative enough. Maybe they are too busy and I don't have enough of them to do this.

Personal staff members play a number of roles. Which role any individual plays at any given time depends largely on personality variables and on tangible circumstances.

PERSONALITY AND THE IMPACT OF STAFF. The personal style of the senator and the personal characteristics of the staff members who work for him are both different. Different senators have different styles of operating, which are reflected in their relations on substantive matters with their various staff members. Said one staff member for a Republican senator:

I think the legislative effectiveness of an AA or LA is really predicated on the man he works for. His effectiveness or ineffectiveness is directly related to the type of an operation that the senator desires to run. If you have a senator who welcomes legislative ideas, then it may well be that the LA or AA is most effective in setting forth ideas which the senator then puts into some form of legislation and takes to a committee or to the floor. But if a senator is not so interested in initiating his own legislation but wants to be well advised of what is occurring in the legislative field, then the LA or AA become quite effective in the research area.

Another Republican staffer agreed:

The office is designed to carry out the role the senator wants to fill. Some guys don't care about being great legislators, or bad legislators. They like the social life in Washington. Maybe their wives like it. Others are issuing seven press releases and introducing seven bills every day. Others would rather be kibitzers and say, "Joe has a pretty good bill; I would like to help him get it through." They don't care whether they get any publicity out of it.

The personality of the individual staff member is also important. An aggressive staff member can increase his legislative impact regardless of the personal style of his senator. Said one Republican staff member:

I think a good legislative assistant can make himself indispensable by the way he presents legislative matters. I think anticipating what is going to come up and being prepared to present facts to the senator makes you indispensable and he becomes receptive. He starts working with you if you show what you can do for him.

Another Republican staffer expanded the point:

A good legislative assistant can in fact become a dominant voice in the office in terms not only of legislative ideas but in making sure that the senator is always well informed as to what is occurring in committee or in floor action.

If a staff man argues with his senator from time to time, this can increase his influence. Said one Republican:

I think the biggest job that an administrative or legislative assistant has is not to be a yes man. He should, if he knows anything about the bill that the senator has been sold on by somebody else, have the courage to go in and say, "That is not the whole story." I have lost most of the battles that way, but I have won a few, too.

Two attributes of the personal style of a staff member are particularly important in helping to determine the amount of legislative impact he can have. First, he can exert considerable influence if he is skillful at providing his senator with the right information at the right time. As one Democratic staff member put it:

You can often think of factors they haven't thought of. Any other human being can if you are working on the same proposition. It is not a matter of personally influencing them, it is a matter of marshalling the facts and mentioning factors that maybe wouldn't have occurred to them, because they are all human and can't think of everything. So to that extent if you do your job you can have an effect.

A Republican agreed:

At those crucial moments when party discipline or party loyalty are not overwhelming factors, then the assistant does play a role in at least providing selective information. The member might not have other information. At a moment of decision, the assistant quickly has to screen out what he thinks is relevant and important for his senator. That alone may determine the outcome.

Timing is often critical. A staff member can maximize his impact by knowing when his senator will feel the greatest need for information. A Republican staff member stated his own formula for acquiring influence:

At the point when a senator gets to a committee meeting, particularly the executive sessions, and at the point when he goes to the floor to listen to the last few chords of debate and cast a vote, there an assistant who is either well read or at least well prepared and is able to pick out the salient points and say which does what to whom, when and how can make a big difference in the final decision of the senator.

Information on new problems, those which the senator may not have faced before, is also critical.

Useful political information or suggestions from staff members also has potentially great impact. A Republican staff member amplified this point:

I think any senator can get carried away at times with an issue. At that point somebody on the staff has to say, "Yes, but you are going politically wrong." I think a lot of this depends on the character of the senator. I worked for a senator who was not politically minded as such. He was defeated. I think in those kinds of cases the staff has to be even more politically attuned.

A personal staff member can usually have his greatest impact on matters of secondary importance to his senator or on those coming before a committee on which he does not sit. Thus, reliable information on these matters is likely to be especially influential. One Republican staffer elaborated:

On the big issues I don't have to tell my boss how to vote. On an issue like civil rights he is going to be voting one way regardless of what you say on a particular amendment. I think where an assistant has the most influence is on a highly complicated piece of legislation that does not concern the senator's committee, that really only comes up once in four years, and it might be a very small piece of legislation. This is where you have influence. This stuff is complicated and nobody knows about it and it might go through on the Consent Calendar. I think most guys are searching for information. If you have facts and information you can have an impact.

Second, personal staff members can have some legislative impact because of the relations they develop with other staff members. If a staff member can persuade other staff members in other offices to join him in urging a certain position on their senators, especially on matters on which the senators are not likely to be well informed personally, their chances of success are high. Patterns of cooperation develop and clusters of staff members can thus develop fairly reliable influence.

OTHER CONDITIONS FOR IMPACT. Three more tangible factors are perceived by staff members of both parties as helping to determine the amount of influence any individual personal staff member is likely to have. First, the personal staff of a senator in the minority party can usually have a greater legislative impact than the staff of a majority senator. One principal reason for this is that minority senators receive little or no aid from committee staffs. Their personal staffs must undertake numerous legislative enterprises that would fall to committee staffs if they were in the majority. A Republican staff member also argued that the minority party has a pioneering legislative role to play in which staff can be important:

A lot of legislation which never gets acted upon as introduced by a minority member does later get picked up by the administration. It is ahead of its time. It is a way of opening up an issue. People start thinking about it. Support gets amassed for it. Assistants working for senators who are interested in this kind of function can have a very creative role. The minority has this role of acting in a creative way and it is one of the last vestiges of creativity left on the Hill apart from tinkering with legislation sent up from downtown.

Second, the seniority position of the individual senator influences the legislative impact of his staff. Democratic staff members agreed that the staff of a junior senator generally deals with a broader range of legislative topics than a senior senator's staff. Junior senators experiment with different substantive areas in an effort to carve out legislative niches for themselves. Senior senators already have their niches. Senior senators are also likely to have committee staff on whom they rely for legislative advice. Furthermore, senior members are likely to have made up their minds on a broad range of subjects and are not particularly subject to influence from a staff member.

But, since staff members work with each other as well as with their own senator, staff members for senior senators, and especially staff members who are themselves senior, are inclined to have the greatest legislative impact, although they may not be dealing with as wide a range of issues as their junior colleagues. Senior staff members, like senior senators, realize keenly the importance of mutual helpfulness in the legislative endeavor. This realization also helps a senior staffer, especially if he works for a senior senator, to increase his impact.

Third, the staff of a senator from a small state has a greater chance to work on legislative matters than the staff of a senator from a larger state. The volume of mail in the office of a large state senator prevents most staff members from having time for much legislative work. The large-state offices may receive several thousand pieces of mail daily, all of which require some kind of answer. Likewise, the large states that are relatively near Washington—New York and Pennsylvania, for example—send a steady stream of constituents to see the senators or their top staff members personally. Naturally, the senators try to content the constituents by allotting staff time to them. Offices of small state senators, especially those from states relatively far removed geographically, are under less pressure from the mail and from constituents.

Senators from the more heavily populated states have more clerk-hire allowance than senators from less heavily populated states, but most of the additional money is taken up by secretaries and clerks, designated primarily to handle the mail. Thus, almost every senator, regardless of the state from which he comes, has about the same number of top professional assistants. These men in the large-state offices must give a substantial portion of their time to routine matters; in small-state offices they are more likely to have their time free for legislative matters.[6]

COMMITTEE STAFF

Partisanship and the nature of the responsibility to committee chairmen and other committee members are the most important factors that help determine the role and legislative impact of committee staff members. Although a distinction is commonly made between professional staff and partisan staff, the distinction is not clear or consistently meaningful. These are not mutually exclusive designations: partisan staff members can also be professionals of the highest quality; professionals can be appointed and retained at least partially on the basis of partisan considerations.

Only one committee at present, Foreign Relations, maintains a staff free of party (majority/minority) designations for specific staff positions. Other committees, however, retain staff members without consistent regard to their party affiliation after they have proven their competence. Said one senior committee staff member:

I think there is some difference between hiring and retaining. I have the impression that the Judiciary Committee staff is as close to professional as any around. I think most of them have been inherited from one or two or three chairmen. I think it is true around the Banking and Currency Committee that folks are retained on quite a professional basis, although they might not be hired anew that way.

Some committee staff members have partisan duties. Said one committee staff member:

In our committee we have a number of staff people who are partisan and they are used on politically sensitive matters by the members of the committee, consulted about it and their opinions relied on. I think if they weren't there, there would be a very definite lack. The senators expect partisan advice in certain matters.

But not all committee staffs provide partisan help. A personal staff member for a junior senator commented:

On Appropriations, for instance, there is a question of who we can talk to in a sensitive area. We have a problem on the extent to which we can sit down and discuss a political problem with a professional staff member more readily than the man with seniority. Obviously a man with seniority has already picked his man on a committee. But the junior senators are seeking out advice from counsel and initiating legislative ideas. We need someone on the committee that we can talk to about issues involving our state that are also political. We need to know how far we can go within the framework of the committee. We have no other means of doing so other than seeking out this man who is both a professional and a partisan.

The Responsibility of Committee Staff Members

The individualistic distribution of power in the present Senate has not permeated the relationship between committee staff members and senior committee members, especially the chairmen. On most of the committees, most of the professional staff members are directly responsible only to the chairman. He appoints them and they retain their jobs only so long as they please him with their efforts. They tend to share his political coloration as well as his formal party affiliation. A few of the staff members may not have this special relationship with the chairman; but they are likely to have a similar relationship with the ranking minority member or, in a few cases, another senior member of the committee, probably a member of the majority party.

All of the round table participants affirmed that the typical relationship was the one described. Virtually all of them, except the majority staff members themselves, agreed that such a situation of limited responsibility (a vestige of decentralized power) inhibited the development of high quality staff work on the committees. The Democratic staff members, since they had gained the most out of the present arrangement (along with the committee chairmen themselves), were more disposed to defend it.

THE DEMOCRATIC EXPERIENCE. Democratic senators at the round tables were not impressed with the job done by committee staffs. They compared them unfavorably to their own personal staffs. Said one:

My observation is that the committee staff people have relatively little to do. You can walk down in the committee office most any time in the afternoon, and they may be reading some things, but they are damned sure getting their hats on ready to go at five o'clock. The people in my office are still throwing it out off both shoulders at six o'clock. The people in the office do a hell of a lot more than the committee staffs do.

Another agreed:

That is right, but the committee staffs ought to do a lot more about digging into their own business of giving you a simplified bit of information. I have been trying for three days to get the number of bills sent in before our committee in brief form, and all I get is the calendar. I want to know what the bills do and what is behind them, and all that. We have got, I guess, eight guys working on the committee.

The principal reason offered for low quality of committee staffs was that most committee chairmen keep the majority staff assignments completely to themselves or parcel out the majority committee slots to the few most senior Democrats. One Democratic committee chairman described the pressures to handle staff in this manner, and protested against it:

On my committee I have had about half the members come in and they want more staff. They say, "I need a staff assistant to be assigned to my office." That is what happens to your staffing. Apparently members have been promised and have used the committee staffs full time in their own offices. This is unfair. The senior senators take this staff, and the new members, who need it probably twice as much, don't get it.

A member of the Appropriations Committee and chairman of one of its subcommittees described the particularly acute problem on that committee:

We have only one guy generally assigned to each subcommittee and he has knowledge of most of the hanky-panky and everything that goes on in the subcommittee, but he doesn't communicate with anybody except the chairman. I know this because I finally got to be a chairman, so I can get anything I want now. But he doesn't communicate with the other members, and yet there are only five or six of them. This guy should be chasing around—because he is not too busy before you start the hearings —finding out what the members want to know and looking it up and giving them some hunches, so when these bureaucrats come down, the members don't just hit the hearings absolutely cold. We don't have any coaching from the committee staff, and that is the reason I want to go out and expand the committee staff on Appropriations, so we will feed back to the individual members some working knowledge of what questions to ask when these guys come in from the bureaus.

Two relatively junior Democrats expressed their resentment at the handling of committee staff and its complete subservience to the chairman:

A: I can't get a committee staff member to do a thing.
B: I don't know who hires. I don't know who they work for.
A: You send letters over to them, and they don't answer them. You say, "What about the material that has come up in the committee?" and they don't give it to you until it comes over on your desk, the day it is up in committee.
B: I think it is a damned disgrace the way committee staffs are hired and supervised.
A: I just don't see how you can get along with your staff unless you are a committee chairman.

B: As a matter of fact, I don't even know the names of all of them, and this is seven years later. You have no connection with the committee staff. They work for the chairman, and that is all.

The Democratic senators agreed that two courses of action were necessary to correct the situation they described. First, committee chairmen should recognize that committee staff members are and should be for the use of all members of the committee, not just the chairman and his senior cronies. Second, the senators could get better service if each senator were more aggressive in asking help from the staffs of committees on which he serves.

Some Democratic staff members asserted that the committee staff man's primary job is to serve and please the chairman:

A: There may be exceptions, but generally the chairman would want his top echelon staff people to represent in the first instance a right political viewpoint. Can you imagine Senator Eastland hiring someone from Senator Hart's office, for instance, to be his chief clerk.
B: I don't think you will ever find anybody who is the chief clerk or the head of the staff, whatever he is called, who doesn't have the confidence of the chairman.
C: On my committee I hope I continue to express the views of the majority, the chairman. If I don't, I am in serious trouble, or else some adjustment will be made.

The influence of the chairman extends even to subcommittee staffs that are formally appointed by another senator on the majority side of the committee. According to one man, senators who have newly achieved the status of subcommittee chairman will pick

somebody who can dissimulate to a certain degree, which will make the person acceptable to the parent committee and the chairman and the staff people of the parent committee. This is a very delicate kind of thing. I think this is especially true of the class of '58. They learned their lesson with respect to dissimulating opinions and accommodating themselves to senior people with whom they didn't agree quite frequently and when they reached the point where they picked up a chairmanship of a subcommittee on a committee chaired by a senior Democrat who might be of more conservative persuasion, they would select people who got along well and who knew how to roll with the punches, who were not blatantly different. I don't think they would select a raving partisan. He may have a viewpoint, but he is very careful about how he expresses it, vis-à-vis the chairman of the committee and the staff of the parent committee.

Despite the agreement that, as a matter of fact, committee staff members are dominated by chairmen and that perhaps this situation is inevitable, there was some disagreement over its meaning. One position was that in most cases the chairman of a committee actually represented the policy viewpoints of the majority of the majority members on the committee. Thus his control of committee staff presented no particular problems, except at the personal level.

A more widely accepted position, however, was that many chairmen have policy views that differ markedly from those of the majority of the Democrats on their committees. When one man suggested that some staff members look on themselves as servants of all committee members and take into account all viewpoints represented, another replied:

Isn't this a self-serving theory that staff members perhaps have promulgated to protect themselves. I think the fact that there is a proliferation of subcommittees shows there is a desire on the part of the junior members to have people they can rely upon, instead of people who "represent" the chairman of the committee. There are some members on the majority side who are very under-represented on committee staffs.

THE REPUBLICAN EXPERIENCE. On most committees, the chairman allows the ranking Republican to appoint whatever staff is allotted to the minority party. Typically these staff members feel responsible only to the ranking Republican. This situation often creates problems.

On one committee, for example, the Republicans had four staff members. When a turnover in the ranking minority member occurred, a bitter fight ensued over the appointment of the four staff members. A compromise of sorts was fashioned whereby the ranking member appointed three, and the next-ranking member appointed one. A senator on that committee described what happened:

The new ranking member, and I think he is probably within his legal prerogative, wanted to have the right to fire everybody on the minority staff and hire those he wanted to have. The second ranking member wanted to fight for one of the fellows who was then on the staff, and did put up a fight. The other three of us happened to agree with the second-ranking man. It became very difficult for the staff member to stay where he was, so he finally moved out. I thought this had resolved the question, but it hadn't, because then it developed that the second-ranking senator wanted to get his own man on. We finally worked out a compromise, but it took an awful long while, and it was a case of a lot of hassling, which I thought was rather useless.

A Republican senator described the situation on another committee:

We only have two on the Republican side that I know of, and they are both working for the ranking man [with whom this particular senator did not agree on policy matters], so I have absolutely no idea whether we have a staff or not.

Republican staff members at the round tables agreed that in many cases minority committee staff members felt responsible only to the ranking Republican. They viewed this as an unfortunate situation and, unlike the Democrats, as remediable.

In some instances the ranking Republican insists on retaining essentially incompetent minority staff members. Two Republicans discussed the sole minority staffer on one committee:

A: The minority staff man works for the ranking Republican member of the committee, and I am not sure that he tells time well.
B: We have been on the committee five years and I have yet to go to him and ask him anything. We have a different problem than the majority. You can have fifteen majority members and have eight of them incompetent and you are still going to get something done. We have one and if he is incompetent, we are dead.

Several Republicans discussed the particularly annoying problem of having individual senior Republicans siphon off the minority committee staff for personal chores:

A: There are cases where a senator doesn't feel he has a large enough staff in his office and uses a committee appointment that comes up for him and the appointee is used thereafter not for committee work.
B: We have one committee man on this committee and he is taken by the individual members. That is one spot we can't call upon for help. We appoint too many political hacks or friends of the family or whatever.

The same situation does not prevail in all committees, however. Some committee staff members try hard to serve all Republicans, at least those who ask for help. Even in a committee that had experienced a bitter fight over minority staff appointments, there was testimony that both the deposed staff members (who had been the appointees of a conservative Republican who left the Senate) and the new staff members (who were the appointees of the liberal Republican who inherited the ranking position on the committee) tried to serve all Republicans on the committee.

One personal staff member for a liberal Republican discussed the former top Republican staff member on the committee (the conservative): "He could disagree with you and yet he could take a look at your state and say, 'Well now, if I were your boss in your state, this is what I would do, or this is how I would answer this particular bit of mail on this thing,' and would tolerate your viewpoint even though he disagreed with it."

The new chief of staff for the minority (the appointee of the liberal senator) spoke for himself:

I am pleased when we get requests for information from offices with which we are not ideologically close. I know they are respecting the fact that we are giving them straight information. I think all staff people should, no matter what their patron's particular point of view is, give as full and factual information as possible.

However, another staff member whose senator became ranking member on a committee—succeeding a Republican quite different in outlook and philosophy—revealed the natural pressures that make a new staff responsive chiefly to the man who appointed them and not to Republicans of different hues:

We have pleasant relations with the committee minority staff now because we have appointed all of them. I must say that I could hardly wait to clean that nest out because we just didn't speak to them for two years. We got nothing but having our projects undercut by a Republican minority staff over there.

The Special Problems of Minority Status

The principal problem faced by the minority senators in relation to committee staffs is that there are very few minority staff members. In 1965, for example, out of 482 staff members on all Senate committees only 73 were assigned to the minority. Even this number represented some improvement over the situation in 1962 when the minority controlled 54 out of 508 staff appointments. Table XX shows the majority-minority split in 1965 by committee.[7]

Republicans at the round tables felt that they were shockingly understaffed on committees and that most Democrats had a deliberate policy of keeping them in this position. Four Republican staff members discussed the pressures of being so few:

A: There are just not the bodies within the staff on the minority side.
B: When I first came on my subcommittee there was only one more Democrat than Republican senator on it, but on that staff they had about thirty-eight majority people and we had two minority people. When you have two against thirty-eight and you don't have any traveling expenses or investigators, you are going to find the minority is in a hell of a spot in trying to keep the senators on the subcommittee informed and making the record in the subcommittee. We have kept pecking at this problem and we have got our minority up to eight and the majority reduced to about thirty. It is impossible for a minority staff to be able to compete, especially where there is a great political cleavage between the majority and minority.
C: For several years I was the only Republican on a staff that participated in legislative activity. During all those years I had to keep my nose in everything, which meant I couldn't specialize in a damned thing, but I had to do the best I could on every single item so if we had any questions come up from the Republican members, I could at least answer the questions and maybe give them some ideas.

TABLE XX: MAJORITY AND MINORITY STAFF MEMBERS
ON SENATE COMMITTEES, 1965

COMMITTEE	TOTAL STAFF	MAJORITY	MINORITY
Aeronautical and Space Sciences	16	14	2
Agriculture and Forestry	7	5	2
Appropriations	35	32	3
Armed Services	17	14	3
Banking and Currency	20	16	4
Commerce	32	28	4
District of Columbia	10	8	2
Finance	6	6	0
Foreign Relations [a]	20	—	—
Government Operations	56	48	8
Interior and Insular Affairs	14	11	3
Judiciary	137	116	21
Labor and Public Welfare	28	23	5
Post Office and Civil Service	15	13	2
Public Works	13	10	3
Rules and Administration	22	17	5
Select: Small Business	20	18	2
Select: Aging	14	10	4
Total	482	389	73

[a] The Foreign Relations Committee staff is appointed without regard to party affiliation.

D: Even with four minority people—and I think we have one of the best majority-minority ratios in the Senate—we find ourselves undermanned, because we get hearings or executive sessions going in several of our permanent subcommittees at the same time. Then we have a couple of *ad hoc* subcommittees, so we find we have hearings or executive sessions going in them too.

Given the lack of many staff members directly responsible to the minority, Republican senators and staff members explore the majority staff for whatever help it can offer. Their experience has been mixed.

Even the one "nonpartisan" staff—that on Foreign Relations—

did not prove satisfactory to all Republicans all of the time. Some felt that the staff members were, in effect, captives of the State Department, more intent on preserving good relations with the Administration than on offering independent views and information. Republican staff members voiced differing views: One man said, "We have had nothing but the best of cooperation with the people there." A staff member for another senator disagreed:

We get a lot of complaints from people not on the committee and they call us to get the information for them. Our senator is on it. When other Republicans have to call us because they aren't getting much cooperation, there is something wrong. They always tell you they are nonpartisan, but I think they slant things the administration way.

Another man agreed with this dim view of the "nonpartisan staff" on Foreign Relations:

If I can get the man I want there it is very fine, but some of the others give you the slickest brush-off and say, "We have never done a study on that." They are just lying in their teeth. Another guy who is a square shooter will say, "Sure, we have something here," and will send it right over. It is not an even group. Some of them are highly partisan.

Experience also varied with staff members clearly labeled Democratic. One Republican senator evidenced a lack of trust in the judgment of committee staff members of either party:

I am absolutely positive that in many instances my staff knows the committee staff people pretty well, on both sides. They know on whom they can rely and they know which one to deal with on a particular subject. But I don't do it personally. My own staff people come back and report to me, including their own analysis of the information that they have been able to pick up. So that I can't say the minority and majority staffs are necessarily sour, any of them. All I can say is that I prefer to work through my own staff.

Another Republican said that on one of his committees there were two minority employees, both of whom he trusted. On the majority side he trusted the chief staff member, but as for the rest of them: "I never go near them."

Some Republican staff members said they could not rely on or even trust the Democratic staff on some committees. Others indicated that they could rely on the majority staff—or at least some individuals on it—for routine information and for honest answers to questions, but that they would not expect the majority staff to go beyond the specific question asked. None indicated that he relied heavily and constantly on a majority staff member for help on sensitive problems.

The Quality of Committee Staffing

Evidence on the quality of committee staffing is scanty. What there is suggests that the situation varied radically from committee to committee and even from one subcommittee to another within a single committee. It also varies over time. A committee with a weak staff is capable of developing a strong staff and then again dissipating its resources.

On the Banking and Currency Committee, for example, the staff of the Housing Subcommittee was so much stronger a few years ago than the staff of other subcommittees that the agencies under the jurisdiction of that subcommittee received much more thorough scrutiny than the other agencies for which the full committee was responsible.[8]

A detailed study of the Senate Appropriations Committee concluded that the committee staff was competent and professional but undermanned and, until 1966, underpaid. In the view of the author, Stephen Horn, two great lacks remained. First, the staffs of the various subcommittees made no attempt to coordinate their activities so that they would facilitate a comparative judgment on the relative priorities between the items in the different appropriations bills. This situation, of course, reflected the organization of the committee itself and the distribution of power within it that makes each subcommittee chairman almost autonomous. Second, the author felt that the committee should possess a special investigative staff to pursue some of the matters that it uncovers.[9]

Another study that has considered the problem of professional staffing on committees in both houses concludes that committee staffs are capable of "intelligence, integration, innovation, and influence." To varying degrees on different committees, staff members have these important impacts. But the study also indicates that there are many constraints on what staff members can accomplish. They are, first, limited by "legislative norms," which include "limited advocacy, chairman loyalty, deference, anonymity, specialization, and limited partisanship." Second, they are limited by the presence or absence of "committee leadership" by the members themselves. "Staff organization, partisanship, isolation, and specialization" are other limits on what committee staffs can accomplish.[10]

Empirical data suggest that the constraints are such that members rely only slightly on the legislative efforts of committee staff members. Unfortunately, available data that even approach comprehensiveness are on the House and not on the Senate, and thus only inferences can be drawn.[11] The inescapable conclusion to which these data point is that committee staff members play only a minor role in aiding members of the House engaged in legislative activity. Although no similar data are available, the conclusion reached by one close observer is that although Senate committee staff members feel they are more influential than House staff members, "this may be a delusion" and Senate staffers may be "further away from power than members of House staffs."[12]

At least it is safe to say that there is a gap between the actual power of Senate committee staff members and their perception of their own power. It also seems safe to say that they are less influential on legislative matters than personal staff members, although a few individuals with the complete confidence of a chairman will develop considerable, and often visible, influence.

SUMMARY

Senate staff members can become influential on legislative matters because almost every senator has a substantial amount of legislative influence. The demands on the time of senators force them to delegate some of their responsibility and influence to personal staff members. Senior senators may make similar delegations to committee staffers.

Differences of opinion about the relationship between senators and staff members reveal additional aspects of the struggle for power in the Senate. Virtually all senators would like more personal staff to help them strengthen their hold on their seats and their reputations as experts in specific substantive areas, but junior senatore are more eager for this aid than senior senators. In addition, relatively junior senators prefer that committee staffs be responsive to the whole membership of committees. The senior men generally feel that committee staff members should be responsive only to chairmen and ranking members personally.

Most personal staff members have acquired a stake in the continued existence of an individualistic distribution of power. Some of their activities reinforce those of senators determined to prevent a return to either a centralized or decentralized distribution of power. Committee staff members are more ambivalent. Their world is still part of a decentralized pattern of power distribution. They wield power within the confines of this pattern and are unsure what the future would hold if their close personal ties to the chairman or another senior committee member were altered.

Notes

1 The figure 2000 for total Senate staff is an estimate. There are about 1500 members of senators' personal staffs. See Warren H. Butler, "Administering Congress: The Role of Staff," *Public Administration Review,* Vol. 26 (March 1966), p. 4. There are also over 500 committee staff members. See James D. Cochrane,

"Partisan Aspects of Congressional Committee Staffing," *Western Political Quarterly*, Vol. 17 (June 1964), p. 342.

Not included in this estimate are staff employees of joint committees (72 in 1962) and staff members employed by senators in their home districts—probably totalling between 300 and 500.

For other recent commentary on the role of staff see Kenneth Kofmehl, *Professional Staffs of Congress* (Purdue University Studies, 1962).

² Randall B. Ripley, "Congress Supports Clean Air, 1963," in Frederic N. Cleaveland, *Congress and Urban Problems* (Brookings, 1969).

³ John Bibby and Roger Davidson, *On Capitol Hill* (Holt, Rinehart and Winston, 1967), pp. 94-112.

⁴ Royce Hanson, "Congress Catches the Subway: Urban Mass Transit Legislation, 1960-1964," in Cleaveland, *Congress and Urban Problems*.

⁵ Stephen Horn, *Unused Power: A Study of the Senate Committee on Appropriations* (forthcoming).

⁶ For example, in fiscal year 1966 the smallest clerk-hire expenditure for any senatorial office was $88,245 (Quentin Burdick, North Dakota Democrat). The largest expenditure was $254,332 (Robert Kennedy, New York Democrat). Kennedy's expenditures were less than three times as great, although he represented a state with a population almost thirty times as great as Burdick's. Each senator had one administrative assistant; Burdick had one legislative assistant and Kennedy three. Given the pressures on Kennedy's office, it is reasonable to assume that Burdick's top two staff men were likely to have more total hours to spend on legislation than Kennedy's top four men.

⁷ For the data on 1962 see Cochrane, "Partisan Aspects of Congressional Committee Staffing," p. 342. The totals then were 432 Democrats, 54 Republicans, and 22 nonpartisan (Foreign Relations Committee). The 1965 data appearing in Table XX were adapted from a table appearing in *Organization of Congress*, Hearings before the Joint Committee on the Organization of Congress, 89th Cong., 1st sess. (1965), Pt. 2, p. 206. A former staff member for a liberal senator commented that these figures are somewhat misleading because some of the nominal Democratic appointees are really "Dixiecrats" and use their positions and talents to defeat legislation proposed by Democratic Presidents and favored by liberal Democratic senators.

⁸ John F. Bibby, "Committee Characteristics and Legislative Oversight of Administration," *Midwest Journal of Political Science*, Vol. 10 (February 1966), p. 87.

⁹ Horn, *Unused Power*, chapter 5.

¹⁰ Samuel C. Patterson, "Congressional Committee Professional Staffing: Capabilities and Constraints," paper presented at the Planning Conference of the Comparative Administration Group Legislative Services Project, Dec. 8-10, 1967.

¹¹ John S. Saloma III, "The Job of a Congressman: Some Perspectives on Time and Information," unpublished paper, Feb. 15, 1967.

¹² Patterson, "Professional Staffing."

Chapter 9: **Change and the Present Senate**

The future of an institution depends in part on the attitudes of its members toward change. In the mid- and late-1960's most senators were little concerned with planned change or "reform." A few were vitally concerned with individual changes; most were content with little or no change. The satisfactions of life in the contemporary Senate are such for most members that there is no reason for them to question the practices of the institution in which they work. The changes that do find broad favor are aimed at making life more satisfying for the individual senator through the distribution of greater power to him or the increase of power already held.[1] Since an individualistic distribution of power breeds contentment, it is likely to take an outside force or series of events to convince present senators to abandon individualism in favor of either centralization or decentralization.

On those occasions in the last few years when senators have had an opportunity to express themselves critically about their institution, they have done so only in small numbers. Of the 100 senators, only 19 appeared before the Joint Committee on the Organization of Congress in 1965 and 1966. Most of these focused narrowly on one or two topics of special interest. During the Senate floor debate on the 1967 reorganization bill, only four or five senators made continuing major contributions. Most remarks showed little institutional concern or introspection. The thrust of most amendments offered was to enhance the power of individual senators, in part through preserving the autonomy of committees.

Senators concerned about the Senate as an institution and critical of it were overrepresented at the round tables. Yet even they expressed basic satisfaction with the Senate's way of doing things.

THE LEGISLATIVE REORGANIZATION BILL

On March 7, 1967, the Senate passed what it hoped would become the Legislative Reorganization Act of 1967. This bill was based on the recommendations of the Joint Committee on the Organization of the Congress and some refinements added by the Senate Special Committee on the Organization of the Congress, composed of the senators who served on the Joint Committee.

Senator Mike Monroney, Oklahoma Democrat, had introduced a bill in 1966 that reflected the views of the Joint Committee.[2] He made some revisions in his bill after the Senate Special Committee held hearings in August and September, 1966.[3] When this bill reached the Senate floor in early 1967, Monroney accepted a number of additional amendments and saw two that he opposed adopted. Altogether, the Senate adopted thirty-nine amendments to the bill.[4]

The effect of the changes made in the original Monroney Joint Committee bill was to preserve the *status quo*. This reflected, in part, important remnants of the pattern of decentralization that had allowed the senior men on the standing committees to dominate the post-World War II Senate for almost two decades. The resolution establishing the Special Committee provided specifically that it could not report until it gave the opportunity to the standing committee chairmen and ranking minority members to present their views.[5] At the hearings designed to elicit these views, although only three chairmen came in person and another three chairmen and one ranking man sent letters, Monroney felt it necessary to drop two proposed jurisdictional changes: the establishment of a separate Education Committee and the enlargement of the jurisdiction of the Aeronautical and Space Sciences Committee, mostly at the expense of the Commerce Committee. Monroney also felt compelled to change his bill to exempt the Appropriations Committee from the "bill of rights" designed to spread power within committees and make their operations more democratic.

On the floor Monroney accepted a number of amendments weakening provisions for uniform committee procedures. The Senate even passed two amendments, opposed by Monroney and the Special Committee, that specifically left the committees power to proceed as they saw fit.

On the other hand, provisions of the bill designed to help individual senators, provisions such as increased staff allowances, passed easily; restrictive amendments to these sections of the bill were defeated by large margins.

The bill as passed by the Senate was individualistically oriented. Committee autonomy was preserved virtually intact, which, in the present Senate, amounts to a preservation of subcommittee autonomy. In practice, this helps guarantee the importance of individual committee members. Many of the provisions of the bill benefit individual senators directly. These included provisions guaranteeing certain rights in committee, providing additional information for senators, providing additional committee and personal staff, and limiting choice assignments to allow for more even distribution.

ATTITUDES TOWARD CHANGE IN THE PRESENT SENATE [6]

In general, changes proposed for the Senate are aimed at strengthening (or weakening) party leaders, committee chairmen, or individual senators (or the collective Senate). Senators are usually interested in strengthening only themselves. There is almost no interest in strengthening the party leaders. There is substantial feeling that committees should retain a high degree of autonomy, but this is not an effort to give power to the committee chairmen. Rather it is an attempt to disperse power to individual senators through their positions on committees and subcommittees.

The Committee System

SELECTION OF CHAIRMEN. The general lack of interest in altering the seniority system for selecting committee chairmen suggests three possibilities: (1) the chairmen are so powerful that dissent would be severely punished; (2) junior members do not feel threatened by the mode of selecting chairmen; or (3) most senators believe that seniority is the best way (and perhaps the only way) of selecting chairmen. Earlier chapters suggest that the seniority system is tolerable to junior senators because the distribution of power in most committees is widespread enough to offer satisfaction to almost everyone. Furthermore, very few senators feel that any alternative would be any better.

In the Joint Committee's hearings, only five senators mentioned changing the seniority rule. Three favored election of chairmen by each committee because it would be more democratic; two opposed it because it would result in constant logrolling and lobbying within committees.[7] When Senator Joseph Clark, Pennsylvania Democrat, offered a floor amendment to make chairmen elective by each committee, it was disposed of, with almost no discussion, by voice vote. Similarly, senators at the round tables had little interest in changing the seniority system.

ASSIGNMENTS TO COMMITTEES. Senators worry about being burdened by too many assignments. Some have experienced frustrating ineffectiveness from being on too many committees. Some are concerned that every senator be given at least one choice committee as a way of institutionalizing dispersion of power. Round table participants wanted fewer committee assignments and smaller committees.

In the Joint Committee hearings sympathy was expressed for limiting each senator to two assignments and for spreading the choice assignments.[8] There was also some discussion of the practice of having ex officio members of the Appropriations Committee from some (but not all) substantive standing committees on specific appropriations bills.[9] The senior Republican member of the Appropriations Committee, Leverett Saltonstall of Massachusetts, argued that there should be no ex officio members.

The Monroney bill contained a provision reducing the size of some committees and limiting each senator to two major assignments (with exemptions for sitting senators). It also limited each senator to the chairmanship of only one standing, joint, select, or special committee and provided that no senator shall be chairman of more than one subcommittee of each standing committee on which he serves. Present assignments would be exempted, however. The rationale Monroney offered for these provisions shows his desire to spread power to individual senators: "Obviously, every senator cannot be a member of the Senate leadership. Every senator cannot be a committee chairman. But development of leadership within the Senate dictates a diffusion of leadership responsibilities to the maximum extent practicable. Nor is it desirable for members to attempt to direct a multitude of activities simultaneously."[10]

Senator Clark led an effort on the floor to eliminate unequal ex officio representation on the Appropriations Committee. His position was that all committees, and thus all senators, should have equal power. First he offered an amendment to give all committees ex officio members. After that was defeated 63 to 13, he offered an amendment to eliminate all ex officio members. His second amendment was defeated 66 to 17. Monroney explained on the floor that the Joint Committee and his bill did not propose changing present practice because of "the violent opposition on the floor" that it might meet.[11]

Throughout the floor debate on matters dealing with committee membership, all senators were agreed in protecting completely the positions of sitting senators. In this they were more conservative than their predecessors in 1946, who were willing to apply reorganization measures to themselves.

MEETINGS AND HEARINGS. Stress on orderly meetings and announced hearings reveals senatorial interest in giving the individual senator the potential of having substantial legislative impact. Predictable procedure and scheduling allows the individual senator to plan his strategies more carefully than haphazard procedure and scheduling.

The Monroney bill contained a number of provisions making relatively minor standardizations in committee procedure. Monroney, in arguing for these provisions, made clear that one end result of these changes would be to help individual senators by insuring "an adequate flow of information to all committee members on a regular basis."[12] Another member of the Joint Committee, Senator J. Caleb Boggs, Republican of Delaware, made explicit the same motivation: "We would establish more regular rules of procedure for the committees of Congress, and thereby *enhance and make more effective the individual roles of committee members.*"[13]

Even though the Joint Committee and the Monroney bill were solicitous of individual committee autonomy, the Senate, at the urging of Senator Russell Long, Louisiana Democrat and chairman of the Finance Committee, adopted a number of amendments reducing the amount of uniformity required of committees. These amendments specifically provided for continuing the present system of casting proxy votes in committee proceedings, for allowing committees to sit for any purpose while the Senate is in session, for deleting language requiring that all committees print their rules annually (in effect, this allowed some committees to continue operating with no written rules), and for requiring minority witnesses to be heard the same day as majority witnesses if the hearing could thereby be concluded in a single day. Senator Long stated his general position, endorsed by the Senate, quite clearly, "Any action taken by a committee should be discretionary with the committee, no rules should be spelled out for the committee. . . . Wherever a problem exists, it should be worked out quietly by reasoning with the people concerned, rather than by forcing them to have an argument out in the open, where tempers tend to become excited and people find themselves frozen into positions."[14]

The Senate also adopted a series of six amendments proposed by Texas Democrat Ralph Yarborough and agreed to by Monroney, that, in technical ways, reaffirmed committee autonomy. For example, in agreeing to an amendment giving the committees more individual control over televising and broadcasting of hearings, Monroney said,

This amendment deals more or less with the internal decisions of the committee which rightly belong to the committee. . . . [T]he decision . . . should be a part of the internal operation of the committee, and not one of the areas in which the Senate itself should prescribe hard and fast rules.[15]

Monroney's attitude toward committee autonomy in the floor debate was, of necessity, sympathetic. He was forced to agree to most of the amendments offered to weaken the uniform provisions in his bill in order to assure passage of the bill.

Senators at the round tables also exhibited great respect for committee autonomy. None of the participants had any particular concern for changing—or establishing—rules for the standing committees. They regarded despotic chairmen as a problem of the past and felt that most, if not all, committees operated in a reasonable way and usually arrived at democratic decisions on matters about which a majority of the committee really cared.

COMMITTEE STAFF. Most senators want more staff, and they are particularly anxious that it be responsible to them personally, not just to chairmen. In the Joint Committee hearings, nine senators asked for more committee staff or personal staff for use specifically on committee business.[16] None opposed increasing, in some fashion, committee staff help. On the floor, Senator Allen Ellender, Louisiana Democrat, introduced amendments deleting the provisions for additional committee staff members and a review specialist for each committee. These were defeated easily, one by a roll call of 51 to 23, the other by voice vote. No one sided with Ellender in debate.

The round table participants of both parties also wanted the responsibility for committee staff more clearly defined and more democratically distributed. They were not agreed on any single method of doing this. They recognized the legitimacy of some of the claims of chairmen to staff control, but were unwilling to see all committee staff responsive solely to the senior members. They were also unwilling to see committee staff pirated for errand-running and personal work for individual senators. Yet they were unsure how to stop this practice and how to institute corrective measures.

JOINT COMMITTEES. General opposition to the establishment of more joint House-Senate committees is probably motivated by fear that an individual senator (and the Senate as an institution) would lose power to members of the House, who have more time to become expert in relatively narrow subject matter areas. In senatorial testimony before the Joint Committee there was some support for jointly conducted committee hearings, but little support for new formally-established joint committees. On the floor the Senate considered no amendments dealing with joint committees or coordinated committee memberships.

The senators at the round tables were more interested in this subject. The Democratic participants felt that the existing joint committees all work satisfactorily.[17] They agreed that the joint committee device should be more widely used, at least experimentally, but were unable to specify any general rules for establishing new ones. They preferred that any new joint committees possess only advisory or informative power, not legislative power. The Republican participants took a dimmer view of expansion of joint committees, even on an experimental basis. There was general opposition in both parties to joint hearings by already established standing committees in the two houses.

Party Leadership

Senators in the mid-1960's have shown virtually no interest in questions of party leadership. Despite some limited complaining, there is basic satisfaction with the present principal leaders, Mansfield and Dirksen.

In the Joint Committee hearings only Senator Clark spoke about the role of party leadership. He argued for a more disciplined party, but one in which all senators would have a greater voice in taking party positions. He was willing to subordinate the individual senator to the party decision, but only if that individual senator had, through the conference, been given a voice in making the decisions. Those who persisted in voting against the party should be deprived of or denied key committee positions, or denied admission to the conference.

The Monroney bill contained no provisions dealing with party leadership. On the floor only Clark referred to the subject of party leadership. He offered an amendment to provide a new standing rule of the Senate that would bring any item recognized as a "major legislative matter" to the floor regardless of committee inaction. One purpose of the proposed amendment was to strengthen party leaders, linked firmly to the President. His analysis of the present situation is in many ways accurate, yet none of the five senators on the floor at the time that Clark and Monroney debated the amendment agreed with him. said Clark:

> My thesis is that any President of the United States has a right, under the Constitution and under the orderly processes of government, to have a vote on the merits of his major legislative proposals by the whole body of the House or by the whole body of the Senate. . . .
> In addition to the other benefits of this proposed rule . . . it would tend . . . to give the majority leader—who would presumably support the recommendations of the President of the United States when the President is of the same political party—an additional tool over the committee chairman and the other members of the committee which might be "pickling" or bottling up legislation which the President ardently desires. This, in turn, would . . . tend to change the present situation . . . which . . . in many instances, results in the legislative committees being the masters of the Senate, instead of the Senate being the master of its committees—which it creates as its agents.[18]

Oversight of Programs

Senators who favor increasing oversight of government agencies want to increase the power of the Senate as an institution, which, in practice, means increasing the power of individual senators in key committee and subcommittee spots overseeing specific agencies.

There was little discussion of this in the Joint Committee hearings. The provision of the Monroney bill allotting review specialists to the standing committees was aimed at increasing the power of the Senate to oversee programs, and an effort to delete this provision was defeated on the floor.

Oversight of Appropriations

The senators in the round tables were concerned with oversight of the budget and the entire appropriations process. The desire for greater oversight in the area is also prompted by a desire to increase the power of individual senators.

Senators of both parties resented House attitudes toward the place of the Senate in appropriations. The Senate, they felt, should be more than just a court of appeals, but the House tends to cast it in that role and is scornful of the Senate when it increases House appropriation figures.[19]

One senior Democrat and member of the Appropriations Committee expressed the opinion that the Senate should play a more important role in overseeing the Executive branch in the appropriations process rather than letting the House alone explore matters in depth.

The House would like to have us only a Court of Appeals. However, we go into a lot of other things, even though we have but three or four members there. If we had better staffs, more adequately equipped staffs, better accounting procedures, a better listing of the budgets, better knowledge of the carry-over in the year, the Senate could still do a much better job.

One major objective of the Monroney bill was to provide individual members with sufficient information for understanding the budget. Presumably, this would increase the influence of the individual senator. As Senator Boggs explained these provisions, "We would give Congress better tools with which to consider the Federal budget and keep individual Members informed, and thereby to better carry out the essential congressional function of the 'power of the purse.'"[20]

Office Staff and Allowances

The widespread desire for increased staff reflects the wish to strengthen the hand of the individual senator. At the Joint Committee hearings several senators supported provisions for more office staff and allowances for travel and communications. The Monroney bill contained a number of provisions asking for increases. On the floor the Senate defeated attempts to reduce or eliminate increases.

The round table participants from both parties wanted more personal staff. They felt that routine office work threatens to engulf even their top staff members, who need freedom to work both on legislative problems and on significant political problems with which each senator must deal if he is to be effective and, ultimately, if he is to retain his seat.

Floor Procedure

Procedural changes that seem to enhance the power of individual senators by giving them better information on the schedule and use of the rules attract many supporters. Such changes may, of course, limit the power of the committee oligarchs, who can cope better with opposition if their potential opponents do not have access to all the information they do.

At the round tables there was considerable support among the participants for a more regularized floor procedure in the Senate. The Democrats were particularly eager to see floor procedure made less dependent on unanimous consent. At present, if an individual senator considers objecting to some unanimous consent agreement, the Majority Leader is usually successful in talking him out of it. The participants commented that they generally did not know the schedule for floor business even a day ahead of time. Matters often come to the floor before the committee report is available for all members to read. Several comments by four Democrats show the extent of their dissatisfaction:

A: It seems to me this unanimous consent business that we have in the Senate is destroying a whole lot of our rules and I wish somebody would stand up and enforce the rules of the Senate for a few days.

B: I agree with you, with the corollary that you go back to the rules that are a little more reasonable for moving the business along under the rules, rather than always circumventing with the unanimous consent.

A: We have a rule that you can't get a unanimous consent agreement unless there has been a quorum call immediately preceding it. And how many times is that rule obeyed?

B: Never.

C: Some of these days they are going to pass a whing doodle, and everybody will wonder how it got by.

D: The first time I saw Sam Rayburn after I went over to the Senate, he said, "How do you like it, working over there, without rules?"

These Democrats suggested several ways to enforce at least some of the present rules better and make a more orderly process out of Senate floor consideration of legislation. They wanted to have the calendar called in an orderly fashion every other Monday instead of generally being dispensed with. In connection with this, they proposed that the Calendar Review Committee (now called the Legislative Review Committee) resume functioning as it did a few years ago: spotting problems with specific bills and insisting on amendments to rectify the shortcomings. At that time freshman Democrats were on it and had time to pay attention to its work. Now, however, because a seat on the Legislative Review Committee also means a seat on the Policy Committee, more senior Democrats have retained their positions on the former.

The Republicans were much happier with the floor procedure used by the Senate. They attributed the decline in activity of the calendar committees to the more informal style of Mansfield compared to that of Johnson or Knowland, and they saw no particular need to reactivate the committees. With some reservations, they were convinced that unanimous consent agreements were helpful and fair. Several of the more senior Republicans observed that the leaders of both parties checked with the interested individuals before approving a given unanimous consent agreement. One junior Republican countered, however, that, unless a senator were on the substantive committee from which the bill came, he was not likely to be called. There is a procedure in both parties by which an individual senator, *if he knows the schedule in time,* can block floor consideration of a bill by registering a complaint with a staff member to the floor leader.

One Republican who saw some problems in keeping informed of

what was on the calendar had a specific suggestion for a change in practice.[21]

> I don't like to see bills reported out of committees and then taken up just as soon as they have complied with the rules. I would rather see them on the calendar for two or three or four days to give me time to get a copy of a committee report and sometimes the hearings, or to satisfy my mind about it. Sometimes they move a little too fast for me personally.

In general, however, the Republicans were satisfied with floor procedure and with Mansfield's conduct on the floor. Members of both parties think Mansfield is more solicitous of Republicans than of Democrats; in such a situation his popularity with Republicans is not hard to understand.

The Joint Committee's mandate specifically provided that it could not make recommendations about the "rules, parliamentary procedure, practices, and/or precedents" of either house, although it could take testimony in this area.[22] Only a few senators talked about this matter, and only one, Clark, made requests for far-reaching rules changes.[23]

On the floor the only rules change that received much attention was a proposal to outlaw co-sponsorship in almost all cases. This was defeated by roll call, 18 to 48. The opponents were especially anxious to retain co-sponsorship as a device for spreading credit for legislation among various individual senators. They argued that a chairman could pre-empt a bill, but that co-sponsorship at least let those who had done the real work of development retain their names on it.[24]

CONCLUSIONS

The shape of the contemporary Senate is now clear. The distribution of power based on personal skills and institutional positions is predominantly individualistic. Party leaders make few requests of the members; the bargaining position of the individual senators is good, even when weighed against that of the leaders. Senators can use the leaders to help them attain their own individual ends.

Committee chairmen have more power than many nonchairmen, and they have a number of sources both to develop and to maintain their power. But they are not strong enough to threaten the basic independence or substantive power of individual members. They are limited in what they can do by the necessities of the accommodating and consensual style of life that dominates the Senate.

At present every individual senator can, if he so desires, become an acknowledged expert on some specific subject matter. In this area his position will almost always become the position of the entire Senate. The present legislative process in the Senate is characterized by (1) a high degree of specialization by individual senators; (2) a scarcity of information on substance, procedure, and the intentions of others; (3) the widespread belief that mutual helpfulness is indispensable to the functioning of the Senate; (4) the lack of any single dominant force; and (5) a segmented and sporadic (though not necessarily small) flow of legislative business. Even some of the most controversial issues can be disaggregated to the level of individual specialists, although some issues, such as civil rights, cannot be handled this way. Instead they depend more than most issues on the construction of firm and relatively visible coalitions.

Staff members, especially those high on personal staffs, possess considerable power, and they have a stake in the continuation of the individualistic pattern of power distribution. Committee staff members are dependent on committee chairmen or ranking minority members for whatever power they develop. They are remnants of a decentralized Senate and have a stake in maintaining the remaining decentralized features.

The senators themselves are generally willing to consider seriously only those changes or reforms that will benefit themselves. They do not want to strengthen their competitors inside the Senate, although they are willing to acquiesce in the preservation of some elements of decentralized power in the hands of committee chairmen. They do not believe that the demands and needs of those outside the Senate necessitate any changes inside the Senate.

As was suggested at the beginning of Chapter 1, whatever contributes to the thorough, rational, representative, and responsible consideration of legislative proposals and administrative actions is likely to enhance the responsiveness of the Senate to the public interest. Whatever detracts from such consideration decreases the chances of responsiveness to the public interest.

Thoroughness is present in Senate actions if the major aspects of a problem are identified and appraised and the major alternative solutions to the problem are also identified and appraised. Rationality is present if a solution is reached that promises to meet an identified need with some effectiveness. Representativeness is present if the major contending interests are weighed during the decision-making process. Responsibility is present if the agents who have the most influence in making decisions are readily visible. Where responsibility is lacking, arbitrary action is more likely to be invisible and undetected.

No one style of life in the Senate serves the public interest completely and no style completely ignores the public interest. Table XXI summarizes a series of speculative judgments about the impact of the three styles on the thoroughness, rationality, representativeness, and responsibility of the Senate's legislative activity.

Thorough Senate consideration of bills seems most likely in a highly individualized situation. In such a situation, individual senators almost all have the potential of becoming expert on some legislative matter. They are aided by a large number of knowledgeable and independently important staff members. There is more chance that thorough examination will take place under such conditions than when the committees are merely doing the bidding of the party leaders, without independent contributions from individual members or staff members.

The individualistic style of Senate life lends itself to the repre-

TABLE XXI: EFFECT OF DISTRIBUTION OF POWER ON THOROUGHNESS, RATIONALITY, REPRESENTATIVENESS, AND RESPONSIBILITY

RESULTS	STYLE OF SENATE LIFE		
	Centralization	Decentralization	Individualism
Thoroughness	Least likely	More likely	Most likely
Rationality	Not predictable	Not predictable	Not predictable
Representativeness Number of interests	Least likely	Likely	Most likely
Weighing of competing interests	Most likely	Likely	Least likely
Responsibility	Most likely	Moderately likely	Least likely

sentation of the greatest number of interests. With power highly fragmented, each interest has some chance to ally itself with a key subcommittee, individual senator, or staff member and thus become powerfully represented. In a highly centralized situation the interests that are close to the party leaders are represented, but competing interests may not be. On the other hand, since parties have to agree to compromises between interests in order to attract broad electoral support, the centralized situation may lead to a weighing of competing interests before matters reach the Senate floor. Similarly, since an important individual who chairs a subcommittee does not necessarily have to weigh competing interests and, because his judgment usually passes in bill form on the Senate floor, only one interest may dominate a specific, relatively small area of public policy. Perhaps, in the matter of representativeness, the public interest is best served by a decentralized situation, in which the number of interests represented is likely to be great and there is also a good chance that the competing interests will be weighed against one another.

A centralized situation produces the highest degree of responsibility. The party leader or leaders can fairly be held responsible for what the Senate does legislatively (along with the President in the case of his party). These leaders may be arbitrary, but the arbitrariness is highly visible.

There are no clear grounds for judging which of the three situations is most likely to produce rational decisions.

No one of the three styles of Senate life, then, is clearly superior in serving the public interest. Individualism is most likely to provide thorough consideration and action. Decentralization is most likely to provide representative consideration and action. Centralization is most likely to provide responsible consideration and action.

The Senate is likely to change again; but it is unlikely that the motive force for major change will come from within. At present an individualistic distribution of power offers enough satisfactions to most senators to make changes that move toward centralization or decentralization unattractive. Change is probably more likely to occur because of an accident of history: war, depression, or the emergence of a charismatic President or Senate leader. Pressure for change could develop in a public concerned with stressing the values of responsibility and representativeness, but as yet no such pressure has developed.

Notes

[1] See Roger H. Davidson, David M. Kovenock, and Michael K. O'Leary, *Congress in Crisis: Politics and Congressional Reform* (Wadsworth, 1966), pp. 152-154, for a short, but useful, discussion of the "end of the establishment" in the Senate. This helps explain the diminished interest in reform proposals.

[2] S. 3838, 89th Cong. 2nd sess. (1966). See the accompanying report, *Legislative Reorganization Act of 1966*, S. Rept. 1629, 89th Cong., 2nd sess. (1966).

[3] See *Organization of Congress*, Hearings before the Senate Special Committee on the Organization of the Congress, 89th Cong., 2nd sess. (1966); S. 355, 90th Cong., 1st sess. (1967); and *Legislative Reorganization Act of 1967*, S. Rept. 1, 90th Cong., 1st sess. (1967).

[4] For a useful summary of the changes made and rejected on the floor see *Tabulation of Senate Amendments to S. 355 (Jan. 25-Mar. 7, 1967)*, printed for the use of the Joint Committee on the Organization of Congress, 90th Cong., 1st sess. (1967). The bill never became law. It remained stalled in the House

Rules Committee for the remainder of the 90th Congress and died when Congress adjourned in the fall of 1968. Senator Monroney was defeated in the 1968 election, which probably doomed any serious attempts to resuscitate the bill in the 91st Congress.

⁵ S. Res. 293, 89th Cong., 1st sess. (1965). This resolution was introduced on August 15, 1966, by Monroney. The provision guaranteeing the right of committee chairmen and ranking minority members to be heard was inserted by the Committee on Rules and Administration. See S. Rept. 1490, 89th Cong., 2nd sess. (1966).

⁶ The data on senatorial attitudes were collected from the round table sessions and from the public discussions in 1965, 1966, and 1967 surrounding the work of the Joint Committee on the Organization of the Congress. See especially *Organization of Congress*, Hearings before the Joint Committee on the Organization of the Congress, 89th Cong., 1st sess. (1965) [Hereafter cited as *Hearings*]. See also *Organization of Congress*, S. Rept. 1414, 89th Cong., 2nd sess. (1966).

No judgment that any specific changes are either necessary or unnecessary is intended; focusing on change is simply a useful analytical device.

⁷ The three who favored election were Democrats Joseph Clark of Pennsylvania and Frank Moss of Utah and Republican Jacob Javits of New York. The two who opposed election were Republicans Leverett Saltonstall of Massachusetts and Hugh Scott of Pennsylvania.

⁸ Both Clark and Javits supported a two-committee limit.

⁹ For a discussion of present practices involving ex officio members of the Appropriations Committee see Stephen Horn, *Unused Power* (forthcoming). See also Senate Rule XVI.

¹⁰ *Congressional Record* (daily ed.), Jan. 25, 1967, p. S881.

¹¹ *Ibid.*, Jan. 30, 1967, p. S1122.

¹² *Ibid.*, Jan. 25, 1967, p. S874.

¹³ *Ibid.*, Jan. 25, 1967, p. S888. Italics added.

¹⁴ *Ibid.*, Feb. 7, 1967, p. S1697.

¹⁵ *Ibid.*, Feb. 9, 1967, p. S1864.

¹⁶ These were Republicans Gordon Allott of Colorado, Jacob Javits of New York, Thomas Kuchel of California, James Pearson of Kansas, and Hugh Scott of Pennsylvania; and Democrats Birch Bayh of Indiana, Joseph Clark of Pennsylvania, John McClellan of Arkansas, and William Proxmire of Wisconsin.

¹⁷ They specifically mentioned the Joint Committee on Atomic Energy, the Joint Committee on Printing, the Joint Committee on Internal Revenue Taxation, the Joint Committee on the Library of Congress, and the Joint Economic Committee.

¹⁸ *Congressional Record* (daily ed.), Feb. 3, 1967, pp. S1478-1479.

¹⁹ One senior Republican noted, however, that in past years he had known members of the House Appropriations Committee to come to senators on the Appropriations Committee privately and urge them to restore certain funds. For the public record the House members are sometimes overeager to make a stand in favor of "economy."

²⁰ *Congressional Record* (daily ed.), Jan. 25, 1967, p. S888.

[21] Under present rules, appropriations bills are supposed to be on the calendar three days before being considered. Any member can notify his floor leadership of a permanent objection to ignoring this rule, but apparently none have done so.

[22] S. Con. Res. 2, 89th Cong., 1st sess. (1965). Printed in *Hearings*, pp. 1-2.

[23] Kuchel, Scott, and Moss also talked about rules and procedure.

[24] For Monroney's argument on this point see *Congressional Record* (daily ed.), Feb. 16, 1967, p. S2121.

Appendix A: The Brookings Round Tables on the Senate

In 1965, a series of meetings on the Senate was held at the Brookings Institution. Eleven Democratic senators participated in five discussions. Six Republican senators came to another series of five meetings. Fourteen Democratic staff members met twice. Sixteen Republican staff members also met twice. The staff members worked both for committees and for individual senators. The purpose of the meetings was to have senators and staff members discuss the Senate as it is, and to comment on possible changes.

Although the two groups of senators that discussed these problems were not perfectly representative of the whole Senate, there was a broad geographical, age, seniority, and committee spread among the participants. The participants—particularly the Democrats—tended to come from the group of senators that is just coming into substantial power and has expectations of getting a great deal more power within the next few years. There were, however, other participants who spoke from the perspective of the relatively powerless (freshmen) and the already powerful (committee chairmen and ranking minority members).

A short tabular summary (Table XXII) indicates the general representativeness of the senators who were round table participants.

TABLE XXII: REPRESENTATIVENESS OF BROOKINGS ROUND TABLE PARTICIPANTS

ATTRIBUTE	DEMOCRATS		REPUBLICANS	
	Participants (N = 11)	All (N = 68)	Participants (N = 6)	All (N = 32)
Average (mean) age	54	56	61	60
Average (mean) seniority (in years)	5.8	10.2	10.0	9.7
Regional distribution [a] (in percent)				
Northeast	18	15	50	25
Midwest	9	19	0	28
Far West	45	25	33	28
South and Border	27	41	17	19

[a] The Northeast includes New England, New York, New Jersey, and Pennsylvania; the Midwest includes Ohio, Indiana, Michigan, Wisconsin, Illinois, Iowa, Minnesota, North Dakota, South Dakota, Nebraska, and Kansas; the Far West includes Montana, Wyoming, Colorado, New Mexico and all states west of them; the South and Border includes the 11 states of the Confederacy and Delaware, Maryland, West Virginia, Kentucky, Missouri, and Oklahoma.

All sixteen standing committees of the Senate had members participating in the discussions.

Appendix B: Literature on the Post-1869 Senate

In Chapter 1 a chronology is offered that categorizes different time periods in the Senate as most closely approximating one of the three models of power distribution: centralization, decentralization, or individualism. The literature (other than documents and newspapers) on which the judgments reflected in the chronological categorization are based are as follows:

1869-1885: INDIVIDUALISM. By far the best source on this period is David J. Rothman, *Politics and Power in the United States Senate, 1869-1901* (Harvard University Press, 1966). See Chapter 2 of the present volume for a brief discussion of this period.

1885-1905: CENTRALIZATION. Rothman is also the leading source on this period. See also Nathaniel W. Stephenson, *Nelson W.*

Aldrich: A Leader in American Politics (Scribner's, 1930); John R. Lambert, *Arthur Pue Gorman* (Louisiana State University Press, 1953); and Dorothy G. Fowler, *John Coit Spooner: Defender of Presidents* (University Publishers, 1961). See Chapter 2 of the present volume for a brief discussion of this period.

1905-1911: DECENTRALIZATION. In many ways the best single source on this period is Claude G. Bowers, *Beveridge and the Progressive Era* (The Literary Guild, 1932). Other good sources include Stephenson, *Aldrich;* Lambert, *Gorman;* Fowler, *Spooner;* Sam H. Acheson, *Joe Bailey: The Last Democrat* (Macmillan, 1932); David S. Barry, *Forty Years in Washington* (Little, Brown, 1924); Arthur Wallace Dunn, *From Harrison to Harding* (Putnam's, 1922); John A. Garraty, *Henry Cabot Lodge: A Biography* (Knopf, 1953); and Charles W. Thompson, *Party Leaders of the Time* (Dillingham, 1906).

1911-1917: CENTRALIZATION. There is no single source that covers this period satisfactorily. The best sources are Claude G. Bowers, *The Life of John Worth Kern* (Hollenback, 1918); Seward W. Livermore, *Politics is Adjourned: Woodrow Wilson and the War Congress, 1916-1918* (Wesleyan University Press, 1966); George R. Brown, *The Leadership of Congress* (Bobbs-Merrill, 1922); Elston E. Roady, "Party Regularity in the Sixty-Third Congress," (unpublished Ph.D. dissertation, University of Illinois, 1951); Dunn, *Harrison to Harding;* Garraty, *Lodge;* Barry, *Forty Years;* and James Holt, *Congressional Insurgents and the Party System 1909-1916* (Harvard University Press, 1967).

1917-1933: INDIVIDUALISM. Material on this fascinating period is surprisingly thin. The most relevant sources are Brown, *Leadership;* Dunn, *Harrison to Harding;* Garraty, *Lodge;* and James E. Watson, *As I Knew Them* (Bobbs-Merrill, 1936). Material on the late 1920's and early 1930's is especially scarce.

1933-1937: CENTRALIZATION. Until 1968 there was almost a total lack of literature on this period in the Senate, although the literature on the Presidency and on society in general at the same time is vast. In 1968 a book appeared that has made a good start toward filling the gap: James T. Patterson, *Congressional Conservatism and the New Deal* (University of Kentucky Press, 1968). Another useful source is the annual write-up on congressional happenings in the *American Political Science Review*.

1937-1955: DECENTRALIZATION. The literature on this period is not extensive. The best sources are Roland Young, *Congressional Politics in the Second World War* (Columbia University Press, 1956); Allen Drury, *A Senate Journal, 1943-1945* (McGraw-Hill, 1963); Donald R. Matthews, *U.S. Senators and Their World* (University of North Carolina Press, 1960); William S. White, *Citadel* (Harper, 1957); David B. Truman, *The Congressional Party* (Wiley, 1959); and Rowland Evans and Robert Novak, *Lyndon B. Johnson: The Exercise of Power* (New American Library, 1966). See also Chapter 3 of the present volume.

1955-1961: TRANSITION FROM DECENTRALIZATION TO INDIVIDUALISM. See Chapter 3 of this volume and the literature cited therein for an analysis of this period.

1961-1968: INDIVIDUALISM. See Chapters 4 through 9 of this volume and the literature cited therein for an analysis of this period.

Index

241